PHILIP LARKIN: THE MAN AND HIS WORK

Philip Larkin: The Man and his Work

Edited by

DALE SALWAK

Professor of English
Citrus College, California

MACMILLAN
PRESS

First published 1989

Published by
THE MACMILLAN PRESS LTD
Houndmills, Basingstoke, Hampshire RG21 2XS
and London
Companies and representatives
throughout the world

Typeset by Wessex Typesetters
(Division of The Eastern Press Ltd)
Frome, Somerset

Printed in Hong Kong

British Library Cataloguing in Publication Data
Philip Larkin: the man and his work.
1. Larkin, Philip—Criticism and
interpretation
I. Salwak, Dale
821'.914   PR6023.A66Z/
ISBN 0–333–44706–9

In memoriam 1922–85

Contents

Part Three   In Retrospect

List of Plates

1 New library in progress, August 1958
2 Move into the new library, September 1959
3 Official opening of the library, June 1960
4 A study in tranquillity, September 1961
5 Planning stage II of the library, June 1964
6 Philip Larkin, September 1961
7 Philip Larkin with Ted Hughes, May 1975
8 Chairing a talk given by Ted Hughes, May 1975
9 Philip Larkin with Andrew Motion and Douglas Dunn, November 1979
10 Philip Larkin with Barry Bloomfield, November 1979
11 Philip Larkin with Anthony Hedges, March 1981
12 Philip Larkin with Edwin A. Dawes and Dale Salwak, July 1982
13 Commemorating the 80th birthday of Sir Brynmor Jones, October 1983
14 Philip Larkin with Edwin A. Dawes, Sir Brynmor Jones and Sir Roy Marshall, October 1983
15 Philip Larkin with Patti and Dale Salwak, 27 July 1985
16 Philip Larkin, April 1984

Preface

Philip Larkin became an internationally acclaimed figure in the literature of our time. He was known as an exquisite poet, novelist and essayist, as a distinguished librarian, as a man respected and loved alike by his Library staff and academic colleagues. He was, as Barry C. Bloomfield put it, 'always a pleasure to meet and a sorrow to part from'.[1]

In his closing years I came to know Philip Larkin as a friend, and between visits we corresponded frequently. When I saw him on 27 July 1985 he must have suspected that this would be the last time. Several friends had told me that he was unwell; and before Edwin Dawes and my wife and I left his home that Sunday afternoon, he inscribed a gift copy of *All What Jazz* with the words: 'From Philip Larkin in the shade to Dale and Patti in the sun (temporarily and permanently, respectively, we hope)'. On 20 September he wrote in his last letter to me: 'I suppose I am getting better slowly, but the whole business has led to rather a crisis of confidence. To go through the ice of daily life means you can never forget how thin that ice is – you are always listening for the next cracking.'[2]

Sadly, Philip Larkin died at 1.24 a.m., Monday, 2 December 1985 in the Hull Nuffield Hospital. He was buried seven days later in Cottingham Cemetery, after a service at the Church of St Mary the Virgin. In his address, Kingsley Amis spoke for everyone when he said, 'we take seriously what he left us. We are lucky enough to have known him; thousands who didn't and more thousands in the future, will be able to share [his] poems with us.'[3]

Two months later the idea for this book presented itself to me. I wanted to help establish a balanced and widely based tribute to the man and his work that would appeal to all readers. To this end, I wrote to some of his closest friends and colleagues as well as to others who did not know him but could add to our knowledge of his work. The results, gathered here, are eighteen essays in reminiscence and appreciation written especially for the occasion (with only a few exceptions).

I have divided the book into three sections. Part One offers eight sympathetic and firsthand accounts of both the public and the private man. Part Two concentrates primarily on some of the distinctive qualities in his poetry and fiction that have earned him a wide reading public. And Part Three brings the book to a close with four essays about his final days and private vision. Together, I hope the above will give the reader a comprehensive look at the human being whose presence makes the work as highly individual as it is.

Quite obviously this book is a joint endeavour, and it goes without saying that I owe a special debt of gratitude to the contributors. I am also indebted to the following good people for giving me encouragement and professional advice when it was most needed: Professor John Halperin of Vanderbilt University; Professor Stephen C. Moore of the University of Southern California; Professor Edwin A. Dawes and Maeve M. Brennan of the University of Hull; Frances A. Arnold of the Macmillan Press; my wife, Patricia, and my parents, Stanley and Frances H. Salwak. On behalf of Philip Larkin's many friends and admirers, I thank all of them for their efforts, patience and great goodwill.

Barbara Pym has been described as 'one of those authors who keeps sending you things long after you'd thought she'd gone'.[4] I believe the same may be said of Philip Larkin. Although he is gone, we still have the writer, we have the work, and in this volume we have the memories and assessments of some of those people who knew him best.

DALE SALWAK
Glendora and London

Acknowledgements

Grateful acknowledgement is made for permission to reproduce the following copyright material:

Kingsley Amis, Jonathan Clowes and the editor for 'Farewell to a Friend', *Observer*, 19 January 1986, p. 16; John Bayley and the editor for 'On Philip Larkin' (reprinted here as 'Philip Larkin's Inner World'), *The New York Review of Books*, 16 January 1986, pp. 21–2; Barbara Everett and the editor for the second half of 'Philistines' (reprinted here as 'Art and Larkin'), *London Review of Books*, 2 April 1987, pp. 6–8; Donald Hall and the editor for 'Philip Larkin, 1922–85', *The New Criterion*, February 1986, pp. 10–12; X. J. Kennedy and the editor for 'Larkin's Voice', *The New Criterion*, February 1986, pp. 16–17; Hilary Kilmarnock and the editor for 'Poetry: a Personal Memoir of Philip Larkin in his Twenties', reprinted here as Part I of 'A Personal Memoir', *Harpers and Queen*, June 1982, pp. 15–16; David Lodge, Curtis Brown Ltd and Edward Arnold (Publishers) Ltd for 'Philip Larkin', reprinted here as 'Philip Larkin: the Metonymic Muse', in *The Modes of Modern Writing: Metaphor, Metonymy and the Typology of Modern Literature* (1977) pp. 212–20; William Pritchard and the editor for 'Larkin's Presence', *Raritan*, Spring 1987, pp. 62–80.

Extracts from 'Lines on a Young Lady's Photograph Album', 'Places, Loved Ones', 'Coming', 'Dry-Point', 'Next, Please', 'Wants', 'Maiden Name', 'No Road', 'Wires', 'Church Going', 'Toads', 'Poetry of Departures', 'Triple Time', 'I Remember, I Remember', 'Arrivals, Departures' and 'At Grass' from *The Less Deceived* (1954) by permission of the Marvell Press.

Extracts from 'Here', 'Mr Bleaney', 'Nothing To Be Said', 'Broadcast', 'Faith Healing', 'For Sidney Bechet', 'Toads Revisited', 'Take One Home for the Kiddies', 'MCMXIV', 'The Large Cool Store', 'A Study of Reading Habits', 'The Importance of Elsewhere', 'Sunny Prestatyn', 'Dockery and Son', 'Ignorance', 'Essential Beauty', 'Send No Money', 'Afternoons' and 'An Arundel Tomb' from *The Whitsun Weddings* (1964) by permission of Faber and Faber Ltd.

Extracts from 'To the Sea', 'Livings', 'High Windows', 'Friday

Night in the Royal Station Hotel', 'The Old Fools', 'Going, Going', 'The Building', 'Dublinesque', 'This Be the Verse', 'Sad Steps', 'Annus Mirabilis', 'Vers de Société', 'Show Saturday', 'Money' and 'Cut Grass' from *High Windows* (1974) by permission of Faber and Faber Ltd and Farrar, Straus and Giroux, Inc.

Extracts from *All What Jazz: A Record Diary 1961–68* (1970, 1985) by permission of Faber and Faber Ltd; from *Required Writing* (1985) by permission of Farrar, Straus and Giroux, Inc.

Extracts from 'Aubade' (1977) by permission of Faber and Faber Ltd.

Extracts from Philip Larkin's unpublished letters by permission of the Literary Executors of the Estate of Philip Larkin.

Every effort has been made to trace all copyright-holders, but if any have been inadvertently overlooked the publishers will be pleased to make the necessary arrangement at the first opportunity.

Notes on the Contributors

Kingsley Amis was born in South London in 1922 and was educated at the City of London School and at St John's College, Oxford, of which he is an Honorary Fellow. Between 1949 and 1963 he taught at the University College of Swansea (of which he is also an Honorary Fellow), Princeton University and Peterhouse, Cambridge. He started his career as a poet and has continued to write in that medium ever since. His novels include *Lucky Jim*, *Take A Girl Like You*, *The Anti-Death League*, *Ending Up*, *The Alteration*, *Jake's Thing*, *Russian Hide-and-Seek* and *Stanley and the Women*. Among his other publications are *New Maps of Hell*, a survey of science fiction, *Rudyard Kipling and His World* and *The Golden Age of Science Fiction*. He published his *Collected Poems* in 1979 and has also edited *The New Oxford Book of Light Verse* and *The Faber Popular Reciter*. Kingsley Amis was awarded the CBE in 1981 and the Booker Fiction Prize for *The Old Devils* in 1986.

John H. Augustine is currently a Doctoral Dissertation Fellow at the University of Minnesota. A Fulbright Scholar at Merton College, Oxford, 1984–5, he taught in the English Department of Yale University from 1981 to 1984.

John Bayley is Warton Professor of English Literature and Fellow of St Catherine's College, Oxford. His publications include *In Another Country* (novel), *The Romantic Survival: A Study in Poetic Evolution*, *The Characters of Love*, *Tolstoy and the Novel*, *Pushkin: A Comparative Commentary*, *The Uses of Division: Unity and Disharmony in Literature*, *An Essay on Hardy*, *Shakespeare and Tragedy* and a collection of essays, *The Order of Battle at Trafalgar*.

Maeve M. Brennan joined the library staff of the University College of Hull in January 1953 and remained there until she took early retirement in September 1985. Consequently, she was already on the staff when Philip Larkin was appointed Librarian and had the unique privilege of working with him throughout the thirty years he spent at Hull. During that time, she came to know him well, both as a colleague and as a friend.

Anthony Curtis read English at Oxford for two terms in 1944 and 1945, returning in 1948 after service in the Royal Air Force to complete his degree. In 1949 he was awarded the Chancellor's Prize for an English essay. Since then he has worked in journalism and is currently the literary editor of the *Financial Times* (London). His *The Pattern of Maugham* appeared in 1974, and he is editor of *Somerset Maugham: The Critical Heritage* (1987) with John Whitehead.

Edwin A. Dawes is the Reckitt Professor and Head of the Biochemistry Department at the University of Hull. Besides being a distinguished scientist, he is also a noted magic historian and collector. As Chairman of the Library Committee Professor Dawes had the added privilege of working closely with Philip Larkin.

Barbara Everett is Senior Research Fellow at Somerville College, Oxford. She has written on a wide range of literary subjects, including two editions of Shakespeare, *All's Well That Ends Well* and *Antony and Cleopatra*. Her latest publication is *Poets in Their Time*, a selection of her essays on authors from Donne, Marvell and Rochester to Eliot and Larkin.

Donald Hall has published eight books of poems, most recently *Kicking the Leaves* and *The Happy Man*. Some of his prose books include *String Too Short to Be Saved* and *Remembering Poets*, both volumes of reminiscence; three collections of essays about poetry including *The Weather for Poetry*; *Fathers Playing Catch with Sons*, essays on sports; *The Ideal Bakery*, short stories; and *Seasons at Eagle Pond*, essays. He taught for seventeen years at the University of Michigan and has received two Guggenheim Fellowships.

Hazel Holt was born in Birmingham in 1928 and educated at King Edward VI High School. On leaving Cambridge, where she read English, she joined the staff at the International African Institute, where she worked with Barbara Pym for over twenty-five years, eventually taking over from her as Assistant Editor of *Africa*. She is Barbara Pym's Literary Executor and, as such, has prepared for press the typescripts of *An Unsuitable Attachment* (1982), *Crampton Hodnet* (1985) and *An Academic Question* (1986). She also, with Hilary Pym, edited Barbara Pym's letters and diaries, published as *A Very Private Eye* (1984). She is also the editor of an anthology of some of Barbara Pym's unpublished works (*Civil to Strangers*, 1987), and is working on the official biography.

Noel Hughes was born in Coventry in 1921. He was at King Henry VIII School, Coventry, with Philip Larkin. When, in 1940, they both went to St John's College, Oxford, they shared rooms until Hughes joined the Royal Air Force. After the war he turned to journalism, mostly concerned with education and industry, topics on which he broadcast and wrote for *The Times* and its Supplements. Later he became a publisher, a director of Associated Book Publishers with control of its educational, academic, scientific and medical publishing. He is retired and now occupied with making stringed instruments and exercising a Thames skiff.

X. J. Kennedy has been publishing formal verse since *Nude Descending a Staircase* (Lamont Award, 1961). In 1985, *Cross Ties: Selected Poems* received a *Los Angeles Times* Book Award. His reviews and criticism have appeared in *The New York Times Book Review*, *The Times Literary Supplement*, *Dissent*, *The Atlantic*, *The New Republic* and *The New Criterion*. He has written textbooks, including *An Introduction to Poetry* (6th edn, 1986), and edited an anthology of hatred in English poetry, *Tygers of Wrath* (1981). He has taught English at Leeds, California (Irvine), Wellesley, Michigan, North Carolina (Greensboro) and Tufts. At present he is a freelance writer in Bedford, Massachusetts.

Hilary Kilmarnock resides in London with her husband, Lord Kilmarnock. She was formerly married to Kingsley Amis.

David Lodge is Honorary Professor of Modern English Literature at the University of Birmingham. His publications include *Changing Places* and *Small World: An Academic Romance* (novels); and *The Novelist at the Crossroads and Other Essays on Fiction, Language of Fiction, The Modes of Modern Writing*, and *Working with Structuralism: Essays and Reviews on Nineteenth- and Twentieth-Century Literature*. He is a Fellow of the Royal Society of Literature.

Bruce K. Martin is Endowment Professor of the Humanities and Chairman of the English Department at Drake University. In 1986–7 he served as Fulbright Visiting Professor at the University of Singapore. Besides essays on various figures in British and

American literature, he has written a study of Philip Larkin (1978) and *British Poetry since 1939* (1985).

William H. Pritchard is Henry Clay Folger Professor of English at Amherst College. His most recent book is *Frost: A Literary Life Reconsidered*.

Janice Rossen is the author of *The World of Barbara Pym* (1987) and of a forthcoming study of Philip Larkin. She is Assistant Professor of English at Chapman College.

J. R. Watson is Professor of English at the University of Durham. He is the author of a number of books on the Romantic period, including *Wordsworth's Vital Soul* (1982) and *English Poetry of the Romantic Period, 1789–1830* (1985). He is the editor of *Everyman's Book of Victorian Verse* (1982), and author of *The Poetry of Gerard Manley Hopkins* (1987). He has particular interests in the Romantic and Victorian periods, especially in landscape and hymnology.

John White is Senior Lecturer in American History at the University of Hull. He is the author of numerous essays and reviews as well as four books: *Slavery in the American South* (with R. W. Willett), *Reconstruction After the American Civil War*, *Black Leadership in America, 1895–1968*, and *Billie Holiday: Her Life and Times*. He was awarded Fulbright Grants in 1962–4, 1977 and 1984–5.

Dale Salwak (editor) is Professor of English at Southern California's Citrus College. He was educated at Purdue University and the University of Southern California under a National Defense Education Act competitive fellowship programme. His publications include studies of John Wain and A. J. Cronin; reference guides to Kingsley Amis, John Braine, A. J. Cronin, Carl Sandburg and John Wain; and three collections: *Literary Voices: Interviews with Britain's 'Angry Young Men'*, *Mystery Voices: Interviews with British Mystery Writers* and *The Life and Work of Barbara Pym*. Currently he is completing a study of Kingsley Amis, for which he was awarded a grant by the National Endowment for the Humanities. In 1987 Purdue University awarded him its Distinguished Alumnus Award.

Part One
The Man

1

Farewell to a Friend[1]

Kingsley Amis

I met Philip Larkin in my first week at Oxford in the spring term of 1941. In what was to me an outlandish milieu he struck me at once as entirely affable, someone who erected no barriers. Partly perhaps through having been at the place since the previous October he moved in it without awkwardness, even with a touch of the spectacular to be seen in his style of dress: bow ties, check shirts, plum-coloured trousers – no commonplaces then. I was wise enough to know, or thought I knew, that this sort of thing was no sign of any particular artistic bent. Indeed even in our college, St John's, there were almost enough velvet-waistcoated barbarians to suggest the opposite.

In a group, which was where I usually saw him, Philip's manner was sociable, talkative, sometimes noisy, scattered with bursts of laughter and imitations of Oxford stereotypes we had developed in common. (One of these, the Yorkshire Scholar, got into *Jill* under the name of Whitbread.) In fact, to passing acquaintance Philip must have looked and sounded rather like a stereotype himself, the generic Oxford undergraduate of that day or possibly the one before.

His activities and attitudes ran in a similar direction. Drinking was important – beer if available; if not, through wartime shortage, then whatever was there. It went down accompanied by plenty of swearing, belching and hostile accounts of most of the components of our world: dons, porters, lectures, essays, college life, land-ladies, rationing and all the encroachments of the war. Work, English literature according to the English faculty, was a matter for evasion and fraud, confidence trickery to filch a degree. Even a meeting of the English Society, though requiring attendance, was seen largely as an episode in another beery evening or scope for more derision.

Philip's exterior of a non-gamesplaying hearty wobbled rather over jazz. I was ready to meet him half-way, having, like most youngsters of the period, come as far as Benny Goodman, Artie Shaw, Fats Waller and the lesser works of Louis Armstrong without really noticing. With Philip the music was a preoccupation, one I quickly shared. A form ideally suited to those with enough – but no more – music in them to respond intensely to a few strong, simple effects? A world of romance with no guide, no senior person to point the way? Both, no doubt; in any case a marvellous bond and one that endured for many years. With me that youthful 'craze' has never gone away; with Philip, sadly, it dimmed in his last years.

Extra-curricular poetry, in the persons of Hardy, Yeats, Auden and – a recent find – Betjeman, was a permitted subject, and I saw at once that Philip was much more closely concerned with it than I had been, but it was to be mentioned, taken for granted, not discussed. And I was well enough aware that he wrote poetry, but so did I, so did half the people one talked to – superficially, it was no more than might be expected from the likes of us. Even his poems in undergraduate magazines hardly suggested there might be another Philip from the one I had seen.

What brought that home to me was reading *Jill*. The experiences of the hero, John Kemp, in wartime Oxford were instantly attributable to the visible Philip; Kemp's fantasy life, dreamy, romantic, sensitive, seemed the work of a different person. I found them impossible to reconcile – well, so had the author. This set me pondering, and I have hardly finished doing so yet. Only in these past few days have I finally decided that at times there was something strained and overdone about what I saw of Philip at Oxford. He might have been seeing to it that he could not possibly be mistaken for someone inviting intimacy. There was something else about him, a barrier not of his making, that hindered that: his stutter, severe enough in those days to impede conversation, at least in my own case; to discourage, for instance, the asking of questions less straightforward than 'What do you think of Tolkien's lectures?' or 'Are you a Sidney Bechet fan?'.

One day it might be fair to speculate about that childhood of his which he famously called 'a forgotten boredom'. It can be said now that he was and remained a man much driven in upon himself, with increasing deafness from early middle age cruelly emphasising his seclusion. In some ways this may almost have suited him; in others it ran strongly against his remoteness. He was too warm, too humorous, too genuinely sociable – as well as having been a little awkwardly so – to settle into withdrawal. That would have required some degree of self-delusion and Philip was capable of none of that. He extended to himself that sometimes frightening honesty which marked all his dealings with the world and, more even than delicacy of feeling, was a distinctive glory of his poetry.

After the middle of 1942, when I left Oxford for military service, I saw Philip on visits, never prolonged, shorter and rarer as time passed and he settled down in Hull. I never saw enough of him. He remained my best friend and his company brought a jovial reassurance, a sense that the fools and charlatans, the Pounds and Picassos and many of their living heirs were doomed by their own absurdity. But for twenty years and more our chief contact was by letter. Those of his to me brought a tiny, unfading sample of his company lit up by an affection he rarely did more than imply face to face. No wonder he was always the best letter-writer I have known, or that what I will miss most immediately is the sudden sight of the Hull postmark.

But of course, permanently and universally, his poetry tells us everything about him as well as all the other things it does. Visible Philip is there and no mistake – 'Toads', 'I Remember, I Remember', 'A Study of Reading Habits', 'Posterity', 'This Be the Verse' with its over-quoted mum-and-dad opening – and invisible Philip too, strongly, unparaphrasably personal but never self-centred, often amazingly remote and distanced from any interest of his own that could reasonably be inferred by any outsider: 'Wedding-Wind', 'Deception', 'At Grass', 'MCMXIV' – all about those men, nothing about him at all – 'First Sight' – about the lambs in the snow, 'The Explosion'.

Poems like these reduce the rest of us to cloddish wonderment that a man such as we know him to have been should have been able even to think of things like that, let alone set them down with such fidelity, precision and tact: that worthwhile secret is something that neither his poetry nor anything else is ever going to tell us about him. But then this kind of bafflement is a normal response to an artist of the first rank.

Will his work live, will it last? Yes, no doubt about it, if
anything does from this barren time, as, along with much more in
the same strain, I wish I could have told him.

2

Larkin's Oxford

Anthony Curtis

Philip Arthur Larkin became an undergraduate at the University of Oxford at the age of eighteen in the Michaelmas Term of 1940. Great Britain had been at war with Germany and Italy for more than a year but the University continued to run regular arts degree courses in addition to starting shorter courses of six months' residence for service cadets. The composition of the student body in arts subjects was changing through the war; gradually the girls, at that period a minority, would come to outnumber the boys.

> At the end of every term [Larkin wrote] somebody left. Sometimes it was a false alarm: Edward du Cann disappeared in December 1942, waving cheerfully from the back of a taxi, but he was back next term, when he promptly swallowed a pin and was rushed to hospital. But more often it was permanent.[1]

The only men undergraduates granted sufficient deferment to finish their degree courses were medical students and chemists, and those considered unfit for service life, as Larkin was eventually declared to be. Quite why he was granted medical exemption remains something of a mystery. His only obvious disability was a bad stammer.

Before the war in 1938 there were some memorable photographs of the university taken for John Betjeman's cynical guidebook *An Oxford University Chest*[2] by the Hungarian-born photographer L. Moholy-Nagy. In Larkin's first term a bird's-eye view would have shown the city still much as Moholy-Nagy had seen it: architecturally ravishing, the dreaming spires still firmly in place, with black-gowned figures much in evidence; but at ground-level you would have noticed changes. You would have seen lines of sandbags wedged against ancient stones intended to take some of the recoil of exploding bombs and signs indicating air-raid shelters.

Several of the colleges had in part been taken over by the personnel of service ministries. From dusk to dawn the city was subject to the blackout rendering a partygoer's progress through alleys and quadrangles more hazardous than in peacetime. In the small hours some of those elderly dons, who were keeping the academic treadmill turning, could be seen ascending the roofs and bell-towers of their colleges to take a turn of fire-watching; eyes accustomed to interpreting medieval papyri were now on an alert for Luftwaffe bombers that mercifully never came. In preparation for the fire-raids the quadrangles of the colleges contained static water-tanks, like murky swimming-pools, another hazard for the reveller making his way back to his rooms in pitch darkness.

The Michaelmas Term runs from early October to mid-December. As it turned into winter, the elderly don, whiling away the night like Agamemnon's watchman, would probably have been wrapped in several cardigans or sweaters. Those wartime winters in Oxford were bitterly cold. Snow was not uncommon and skating where the river had flooded over Port Meadow an exhilarating pastime. Larkin was not a skater but he did spend a certain amount of time staring at the snow:

> I see a girl dragged by the wrists
> Across a dazzling field of snow,
>
>   .   .   .
>
> There is snow everywhere,
> Snow in one blinding light.
> Even snow smudged in her hair
> As she laughs and struggles, and pretends to fight . . .
>   ('I see a girl dragged by the wrists', XX)

Throughout his writing, both poetry and fiction, Larkin is much concerned with the thought of initiation into full adult experience, belated initiation and complete failure to become initiated. The precondition for initiation is associated in his work with the all-enveloping whiteness of snow. That Larkin had a partiality for poems about snow in cities may be seen in *The Oxford Book of Twentieth-Century English Verse* where he included the poem by Robert Bridges, 'London Snow', and a less well-known poem, 'Snow in the Suburbs', by Hardy.

Larkin had read more widely than most freshmen and had literary ambitions. They pointed him then to fiction rather than poetry. Three years later when he was twenty-one he wrote *Jill* which looked back to that Michaelmas Term of 1940, following the undergraduate career of one John Kemp, a working-class lad from Lancashire who was the first boy ever to go from his school to Oxford. This was not the case with Larkin. Educated at the King Henry VIII School, Coventry, an ancient grammar school foundation, he was not the first boy to go from that school to Oxford nor the last. One of his closest friends at school, Noel Hughes, who contributed some memoirs of their schooldays to the symposium, *Larkin at Sixty*, went up to the same college at the same time as Larkin. They travelled by train from Coventry to Oxford together. In *Jill*, Kemp suffers from acute apprehension and self-consciousness; the thought of being observed eating by the other passengers forces him to go to the lavatory to consume the sandwiches provided by his mother. That hilarious episode did not occur during their journey.

However, this train journey was an important one for Larkin. It was the first time he was travelling as an individual, not as part of a family or school group. Larkin used train journeys by Kemp, from his home to Oxford and back, to frame the action of the novel in the course of which the hero sheds some of his naïvety and gaucheness. When the schoolmaster, Mr Crouch, who encouraged him to go to Oxford, comes up to see Kemp and to talk about his future career, he tells him:

'You can look at this place as a big railway terminus. Thousands of people. Trains starting in every direction. What you've got to decide is, where are *you* going? And having decided, get in with your fellow passengers. They'll be useful to you.'[3]

It was a train journey too which provided Larkin with the material for his most famous poem in which the poet observes, as a solitary, maritally uninitiated figure, the attitudes of the newly-wed and their families, 'The Whitsun Weddings'. And, in Larkin's art at its most mature, 'Dockery and Son', it is on Sheffield railway station late at night, while returning home from a dinner at his old Oxford college, that the poet reviews the whole course of his adult life.

> the ranged
> Joining and parting lines reflect a strong
> Unhindered moon . . .

The moonlit railway track becomes a perfect metaphor for the invisible lines of destiny, briefly tangential then separate, tracing the careers of two Oxford contemporaries, his own and Dockery's. Yet until the Dean mentions that he now has a son at the college, the poet hardly remembers Dockery.

> Was he that withdrawn
> High-collared public-schoolboy, sharing rooms
> With Cartwright who was killed?

These lines open a window on Larkin's Oxford. In 1940 with, as we have seen, some colleges partly taken over by civil servants, room-sharing by undergraduates was not uncommon. Kemp's paralysing self-consciousness continues and worsens, to great comic effect, when he discovers on arriving at the college that he is required to share a set of rooms with an oafish, selfish specimen of the public* school breed. It is perfectly true that St John's, Larkin's college, was at that period short of undergraduate accommodation but, far from being yoked for the duration with a drunken sot from a public school and his cronies, Larkin shared with his schoolmate from Coventry, Noel Hughes. Whereas Kemp's room-mate was obstreperous and inconsiderate, Hughes was quiet and civilised. If from time to time there were unacceptable noise-levels emanating from the room they were more likely to have come from Larkin's wind-up gramophone, belting out his jazz 78s, than from anything to do with Hughes.

Larkin probably had a gratifying sense that at last he was in possession of his own territory, even if for a term or two it was shared territory. For the first time in his life he was well and truly out of the orbit of his father, Sydney Larkin, City Treasurer of Coventry, a local government official much respected by his colleages for his efficiency and high professional standards, much feared by his staff for his ruthless way with incompetence; well-

---

* For American readers unfamiliar with *public* in this British context it implies fee-paying, privileged, 'Ivy League'.

known for choice of a pretty secretary. Larkin *père* was an authoritarian, typical of certain pre-war middle-class Englishmen. The stammer that afflicted Larkin *fils* as an undergraduate soon disappeared after his father's death.

What of Sydney Larkin's literary taste, if any? You would have expected it to centre upon those imperial English writers beloved of the non-literary: Surtees, Kipling, Wodehouse, 'Sapper'; but there you would have been quite wrong. The shelves of the family home in Coventry were crammed with fiction. Sydney Larkin purchased novels in quantities and read them, D. H. Lawrence and 'Saki' were particular favourites. Philip Larkin in a rare fragment of autobiography remembered with gratitude the wide choice of reading he had as a boy:

> Thanks to my father, our house contained not only the principal works of most main English writers in some form or other (admittedly there were exceptions, like Dickens), but also nearly-complete collections of authors my father favoured – Hardy, Bennett, Wilde, Butler and Shaw, and later on Lawrence, Huxley and Katherine Mansfield. Not till I was much older did I realise that most boys of my class were brought up to regard Galsworthy and Chesterton as the apex of modern literature, and to think Somerset Maugham 'a bit hot'.[4]

But it was not from any of these authors that Larkin had a fructifying imaginative experience that released his gift for writing fiction. That came from a novel now hard to come by, *The Senior Commoner* by Julian Hall, published by Martin Secker in 1936. Larkin found it one day on the shelves of the Coventry Central Library.

Julian Henry Hall was the son of a baronet to whose title he succeeded. He was at Eton as a schoolboy and he might well have served as a model for the 'high-collared public-schoolboy' recalled by Larkin in 'Dockery', except that he was up at Oxford at Balliol in the 1930s. He wrote three novels in all, served in Intelligence in the army during the war, after which he was employed in radio as a BBC talks producer, and as an anonymous drama critic on *The Times*; he had a photographic memory for the plays and casts of the pre-war London theatre. In his latter years he devoted much of his energies to the English Association and the Garrick Club. He died in 1974. It seems a pity that he and Larkin never met; one feels they would greatly have enjoyed each other's company. *The Senior Commoner*, which is a novel about Eton (coded as Ayrton in the book), leads one to believe that nothing in Hall's later life ever measured up to his last term at Eton when he became Captain of the Oppidans.

Larkin read Hall's novel when he was a schoolboy and he read it again when he was an adult. 'It is one of the few dozen books I keep in my bedroom', he wrote, 'and can read at any time.'[5] In a short article on it, Larkin began by quoting the final paragraph of the novel which describes the train that is taking the hero away from Eton arriving at its London terminus. As in *Jill*, a railway journey represents one of the few breaks granted to the hero during term from the intense life of the community to which he belongs as a pupil. Although we view the life through the mind of the hero, Harold Weir, we see it sweeping into its continuance other members of that community, head and senior masters, housemasters, prefects and junior boys, even parents. At one point a group of fathers, all of whom are former pupils, are chatting among themselves. One of them remarks to another:

'Junior to you am I? But you've got a boy or a grandson at the place now. I haven't. I haven't got anybody.'[6]

Larkin quoted this to make his point about the seeming irrelevance of much of the conversations and events described in the novel. At the same time he cannot, surely, have been unaware that he was giving away a crucial source for 'Dockery and Son' whose starting point is this situation and which echoes its language.[7]

Apart from whatever contribution it may have made to 'Dockery', *The Senior Commoner* amply demonstrated to Larkin how a novel could be organised around an academic institution. Weir is the natural product of such an institution, completely at ease in conforming to its complex rules and rituals. His eyes fill with tears when he realises that the time has come for him to leave for good. Kemp is the rawest recruit to another institution with just as complex if less coercively imposed rules and rituals. Kemp compensates through inventing and living a fantasy life over which he loses control. In this development Larkin showed power of invention beyond Hall. Kemp's problems all stem from the fact that he went to what used to be called 'the wrong kind of school'. In St John's in Larkin's day from 1940 to 1943 there would have been the usual mixture of undergraduates from both public and state schools, all of them equally preoccupied with the thought of their forthcoming enlistment into the services. The college entrance examination concentrated on ability and it recruited its members from all manner of schools. Many of Larkin's friends and fellow-undergraduates had been to schools no grander or less grand than his. In his mind he made a distinction not so much between public and non-public school as between the bourgeois and the working-class, and his values were those of the bourgeoisie. He was conscious always that, unlike Kemp, his father had paid for him to go to Oxford.

On the other hand Kemp's room-mate was not purely a fantasy figure. There were models for him close enough at hand. The type of brawny rugger-playing public-school undergraduate 'baying for broken glass' we find in early Evelyn Waugh, and the Betjeman book on Oxford already mentioned, was not completely extinct. Noel Hughes tells me that there was one such individual in the college who 'used to get blindingly drunk two or three times a week and bellow his way across the quad. Philip was literally terrified of him'. But not all the public school men at John's were like him, fortunately. For a contrast there was Alan Ross who had been to Haileybury and whose accomplishments included both cricket and writing poetry. Anyone less resembling Kemp's room-mate would be hard to imagine. Ross was reading Modern Languages and shared tutorials with Bruce Montgomery who was also to become a writer. Their tutor was W. G. Moore, later Professor of French at Oxford.

When Montgomery turned to writing detective stories under the name of Edmund Crispin he is said to have used Moore's idiosyncrasies as a model for his regular detective, Gervase Fen. Larkin read English and went to the college's Fellow in that subject, Gavin Bone, with, as his tutorial partner, Norman Iles from Bristol Grammar School. Larkin and Iles hit it off splendidly together. They invented a fantasy character, the Yorkshire Scholar, who became a running gag for several terms. Unfortunately they found their weekly sessions with Bone, an ill man (he died in 1942), much less entertaining. Bone had studied widely in the subject, and was a charming amateur artist; his great passion was Anglo-Saxon poetry which he read 'with very lively pleasure'. One of his aims in life was 'to get this pleasure "through" to the general reader'.[8] In this instance he failed to get much of it through to Larkin.

Then as now at Oxford the student's tête-à-tête with his tutor formed the weekly peak of his academic work, but he was also encouraged to attend some of the lectures given in the faculty by the fellows of other colleges. Larkin would therefore have had the opportunity of going to lectures by a number of eminent dons who were keeping the flag flying in English studies at that time; among them were C. S. Lewis (background lectures on medieval and Renaissance literature which always drew a capacity audience); J. R. R. Tolkien (who had published only *The Hobbit* apart from academic studies of Old and Middle English texts); Nevil Coghill on Chaucer and Shakespeare; M. R. Ridley and Edmund Blunden on the Lake poets. In retrospect it seems a star-studded cast, especially when you add Lewis's friend Charles Williams, the Christian mystical writer from the Oxford University Press, lecturing to a packed auditorium of mainly women undergraduates on Milton; but these dons' enthusiasms did not often coincide with those of Larkin. For instance, neither Hardy nor Yeats were part of his course, which terminated officially with Keats and Shelley. Naturally no one actually forbade him to read *Jude the Obscure* or 'Among Schoolchildren' in his room if he wanted to and to discuss them with Iles or Kingsley Amis or Ian Davie[9] (not to be confused with Donald Davie) or John Wain, all of whom were up at St John's during the war and were writing poetry which they published in undergraduate journals. But Larkin was not required to show any knowledge of Victorian or modern literature in the examination schools.

There were a great many people writing poetry in wartime Oxford, several of them to make a reputation later as poets. They tended to flourish in certain colleges. One was Merton, where Edmund Blunden was the Fellow in English (though not for much longer) and had as his pupil Keith Douglas. Blunden was aware of Douglas's distinctive poetic gifts and tried to help him to get his work published. Douglas and Larkin just missed each other at Oxford. Douglas went down in the Trinity Term 1940 to join the army. The poet at Merton with whom Larkin did coincide was William Bell,[10] a fluent, elegant poet with a mastery of the Spenserian mode. Bell served in the Fleet Air Arm during the war, which he survived and came back to read English, but his passion for mountaineering led to his untimely death on the

Matterhorn in 1948. Bell was important to Larkin because as well as being a poet he was an anthologist who cast his net wide among his contemporaries, as may be seen from the two collections he edited, *Poetry from Oxford in Wartime* and *More Poetry from Oxford in Wartime*.[11] Although Ian Davie had invited Larkin to contribute to *Oxford Poetry, 1942–1943* which he edited, and had published some of his poems there, it was Bell's first anthology which contained no fewer than ten poems by Larkin all of which were later reprinted in *The North Ship*. I first became conscious of Larkin as a distinctive poetic voice when as a Merton undergraduate in 1945 I read Bell's collection.

Another place in Oxford where several of the undergraduates were poets in those days was the Queen's College: John Heath-Stubbs, Sidney Keyes, Drummond Allison were all there and publishing their poetry in the student-edited magazine, *Cherwell*, which appeared during term. Keith Douglas had been editor of *Cherwell* until he went down in 1940. He was succeeded by Michael Meyer, the future translator and biographer of Ibsen and Strindberg, but in those days an undergraduate at Christ Church writing poetry.

> We had a lively team at the *Cherwell* then, [he writes] including, in addition to Keyes, Heath-Stubbs and Allison, Michael Flanders, Philip Larkin, Basil Taylor (later to become a distinguished art critic), John Mortimer and Francis King, with Keith Douglas contributing poems from the army.[12]

Bloomfield[13] lists only three poems by Larkin in 1941 and 1942 in *Cherwell* and this is not surprising because, although Meyer liked his work, Larkin was out of sympathy with the aims of the Queen's poets as they were with his, although both he and they were in reaction against Auden and MacNeice.

Sidney Keyes attempted to define the aims of his group in an anthology which he and Meyer jointly edited, *Eight Oxford Poets*:

> All the poems printed in this book have been written since the beginning of the present war, mainly at Oxford. We have made no attempt however to gather in the whole harvest of Oxford poetry written during those years, but have confined ourselves to a fairly liberal selection from the work of those writers who seem most interesting, most typical, and most hopeful for the

future. Our book is thus rather a group production than a representative anthology; most of the contributors having worked in close touch with each other during the period. Nor is it altogether fanciful, we suggest, to trace certain elements in common to the work of us all. We seem to share a horror at the world's predicament, together with the feeling that we cannot save ourselves without some kind of spiritual readjustment, though the nature of that readjustment may take widely different forms. In technique, there is also some similarity between us; we are all with the possible exception of [J.A.] Shaw, *Romantic* writers, though by that I mean little more than that our greatest fault is a tendency to floridity; and that we have, on the whole, little sympathy with the Audenian school of poets.[14]

Keyes himself, Heath-Stubbs, Douglas, Allison and Meyer were all included but Larkin was not. Although there were two editors the choice of whom to include was ultimately made by Keyes.

I know [writes Meyer again] we disagreed considerably about who should be in. I wanted to include Larkin, among others, and was still dubious about Heath-Stubbs and Allison. In the end he had his way, and I think, apart from Larkin, that he was right.[15]

The declared aims of Keyes and his friends help to delineate the kind of poet Larkin was not. No doubt he shared their 'horror at the world's predicament'; it would have been difficult to discover a responsible adult who did not at that time; but he did not consider the way to overcome it was through Romantic affirmation. In the words of the poem printed in Bell's anthology already quoted, Larkin believed: 'To be that girl! – but that's impossible', and the poem retreats into an examination of the poet's own condition. Keyes and Heath-Stubbs had a vision of universal poetic knowledge; for young men in their twenties they were astonishingly erudite and well-read. Their poems often took the form of a dramatic identification with some admired figure from history or legend, modern life, ancient literature or grand opera. In reviving such a figure in the reader's mind through the poem they felt they were keeping alive the whole tradition of romantic poetry in danger of being extinguished by the war. Larkin's aim, even in his youthful Yeatsian days, was seemingly more modest: the poem as a mode of self-scrutiny.

> In the past
> There has been too much moonlight and self-pity:
> Let us have done with it . . .
>
> ('Love, we must part now', XXIV)

Kingsley Amis was 'junior' to Larkin. The account given by Larkin[16] of how he first became aware of him in the quadrangle as a mimic of genius is too well-known to require reiterating here. They were soon close friends. Amis shared Larkin's antipathy to the learned neo-Romanticism stemming from Queen's, and he shared his love of listening to Sidney Bechet and Pee Wee Russell. Amis also came to share Larkin's admiration for *The Senior Commoner*. Larkin sent him to the Bodleian to check out Hall's other two novels and he reported back that they were not nearly so good.[17] Amis went down in 1942 to join the army, not to return to resume work on his English degree until 1945. John Wain had come up near the end of Larkin's time at Oxford but only remembers having one conversation with him.[18] That left, from the circle of friends at St John's, only Bruce Montgomery, like Larkin exempt from military service. Anyone who has ever sampled one of Edmund Crispin's mystery stories, all of them fastidiously written and full of literary allusive jokes, will not find it hard to understand that he and Larkin should have found delight in each other's company. As Larkin put it:

> I sometimes wonder if Bruce did not constitute for me a curious creative stimulus. For the next three years we were in fairly constant contact, and I wrote continuously as never before or since.[19]

3

Larkin Around in the Library

Edwin A. Dawes

The University of Hull was singularly fortunate to have as its Librarian an internationally acclaimed poet and writer but, inevitably, to the outside world, the glamour of the man of letters eclipsed the more mundane role of the librarian. It was predictable therefore that Philip Larkin's obituaries in the national press would pay scant regard to his eminence as a University Librarian; they were, however, a source of sorrow to his staff and colleagues who knew well the skill and dedication he brought to bear on his daily round. He was understandably irritated when ill-informed commentators referred to him as a 'poet-librarian', implying some curious hybrid existence and raising visions of stanzas being composed while skulking in the stacks. My own friendship with Philip developed as a colleague and, latterly, I had the added pleasure of working closely with him as the Chairman of the Library Committee; it is from this standpoint that these recollections flow.

My first encounter with Philip was in 1963, the statutory appraisal by the Librarian of a new professor, to ascertain his library needs and especially his views on departmental libraries. I quickly discovered that my enthusiasm *for* them was not the 'party line' since, given the very compact nature of the Hull campus, centralised library services were not only feasible but also efficient and economical. Philip left me in no doubt on that score but otherwise was helpful and sympathetic to the requirements of a foundation professor faced with library stocking for his subject. That was the period of expansion of British universities and at Hull the deficiencies of a small, former University College, library were being rapidly rectified. A new library building had been occupied in 1959 and Philip was riding on the crest of a wave of relative affluence, supported by a powerful Library Committee that counted the Vice-Chancellor, and Deans of the Faculties amongst its members. The then Vice-Chancellor, Sir Brynmor Jones, a former Professor of Chemistry in the University, was determined to build up the library facilities at Hull, and generous funding enabled a substantial West Extension to be completed by 1970. The impressive building that resulted bears the title of 'The Brynmor Jones Library' and magnificently reflects the foresight and dedication Brynmor brought to the provision of a library commensurate with the needs of an expanding University; needless to say, Philip Larkin was the initiator of the readily accepted proposal for the naming of the library.

At the presentation following Sir Brynmor's retirement in 1972, Philip observed that seeing him in the library which bears his name was rather like walking through St Pancras Station and meeting St Pancras. It was a joke he economically re-used twelve years later on the occasion of the party to mark the retirement of the Librarian's secretary, Betty Mackereth, when he espied Sir Brynmor in the assembled throng.

Sir Brynmor Jones celebrated his eightieth birthday in 1983 and Philip and I thought that such an auspicious occasion should not be allowed to pass without the Library Committee and members of the library staff paying tribute to his tremendous support for the library. Accordingly a luncheon was held on 26 October. Now Philip did not like making speeches and only if there was no escape route available, such as might be afforded by the Chairman of Library Committee, would he perform. On this occasion I stood firm but, in reality, he required very little persuasion to honour the man who had done so much for the library.

My own association with the Library Committee had first arisen as the Science Faculty representative and subsequently as Dean of Science, from 1968 to 1970. However, in 1967 Philip had conceived the idea of setting up a Library Consultation Board to liaise with academic library users and the student body and he invited me to be its Chairman. Unfortunately it was a rather shortlived venture. The Students' Union nominated as one of its representatives an individual who was a persistent flouter of library regulations, and Philip, together with his library colleagues on the Board, steadfastly refused to sit round the table with such a known miscreant. Despite the Chairman's best endeavours, intransigence prevailed on both sides. Subsequently, after the dust had settled, it did prove possible to resurrect a similar type of committee and one which still flourishes as the Library Users Sub-Committee, reporting to the Library Committee.

Possibly because of these earlier involvements and his awareness of my bibliophilic interests, Philip approached me early in 1974 to ask if he might nominate me for chairmanship of the Library Committee. I acquiesced, and thus began what turned out to be eleven years of close collaboration with Philip. We worked harmoniously and so, as each period of office came to an end (the most recent in the year of Philip's death), he would tell me that he hoped to nominate me again. He could be very persuasive! The reissue of *All What Jazz* in 1985 gave Philip the opportunity to commemorate what he chose to refer to as my 'ten years' hard' by means of his inscription in the copy he gave me.

The Library Committee met in the Committee Room adjacent to the Librarian's office on Monday afternoons, five times per annum. The normal routine involved a briefing meeting between the Chairman, Philip (who served as Secretary to the Committee) and his Deputy Librarian (initially Brenda Moon, and subsequently Tom Graham and then David Baker) on the morning of a Committee meeting to discuss details of the agenda and, where appropriate, to plan any tactics in presentation that were believed necessary. Identification of potentially troublesome members of the Committee in relation to specific business was a matter of course, and we conferred in Philip's office, watched over by the photograph of Guy the Gorilla and stonily eyed by the green toad on his desk. There were inevitable flashes of Larkin humour on these occasions although the ever-tightening financial constraints and the recurring need for the cancellation of subscriptions to periodicals, which assailed us from the mid-1970s, brought sombre aspects too.

Anyone who might have held the notion that Philip was a fey, other-worldly poet would have had such ideas ruthlessly dispelled on first contact at one of these briefing sessions. His mastery of all aspects of library operation (with the single exception of automation, which he came to late in his career) was striking, and his sense of political timing for committees astute. One senior colleague referred to him as being 'wily as a fox'.

Philip always sat on the left of the Chairman at Library Committee meetings. Latterly he wore two hearing aids and occasionally the proceedings would be punctuated by high pitched feedback when he adjusted them to improve reception. Undoubtedly developing deafness placed a considerable strain upon him at these meetings and he would often incline towards the speaker, the better to catch what was being said.

His papers relating to each item on the agenda were contained in a series of files piled prominently on the table before him. Each, in turn, yielded its data and, in response to those agenda items which promised 'The Librarian will speak', he did so in measured tones, emphasising the important points and summarising with great clarity the crucial issues involved. From time to time his discourse would be leavened by an apposite quip, which might raise anything from a smile to a belly laugh.

Invariably for these meetings he wore a sober dark suit with a waistcoat that, over the years, encompassed a gradually increasing girth. 'How do you manage to keep so slim?' he would ask me from time to time, whereupon my own paunch would assume a more deflationary aspect than hitherto. My suggestion that he might exercise by walking to the top (seventh) floor of the West Extension several times a day was met with incredulity.

On non-committee days Philip occasionally wore a sports jacket, although I recall a Library Users' Sub-Committee at which he was thus attired, presumably regarding the agenda as being sufficiently informal to justify his dress.

As might be anticipated, the Library Committee minutes that he wrote were models of style and clarity. The Chairman, a scientist, was always elated if he could detect any errors in the drafts that were submitted for his scrutiny! Now Philip's minutes were invariably extensive and he looked with marked disfavour on the University administration's efforts, several years ago, to streamline minute taking in order to cut down the bulk of paper that was circulated to the Senate. He regarded this bureaucratic directive as an unwarranted attempt to curtail his 'house style' and so continued to produce flowing minutes, characteristically rich in detail.

The last of our briefing meetings remains vividly in my memory. Philip had returned to work on a part-time basis, following his operation during the summer of 1985. The first Library Committee meeting of Session 1985–6 was scheduled for 21 October; a new Vice-Chancellor had just taken up office and would be attending his initial Library Committee, and Philip was not only anxious but far from well. He had difficulty in concentrating, was restless and confided that he wished he didn't feel so wretched. When I returned from lunch, and just prior to the meeting, Philip apologised for having been so unsettling at our morning briefing but claimed now to be feeling rather better. He managed to get through the afternoon without difficulty. Mercifully, it was a short meeting, lasting 90 minutes, during which time he presented various aspects of library business including discussion of the library grant for the session and expenditure on books and periodicals for the previous session.

What, it subsequently transpired, was to be the last Library Committee Philip attended was marked by an especially felicitous quip. The Council of the University had decided to mark the retirement of Vice-Chancellor Sir Roy Marshall, a distinguished laywer, with an award of £5000 for the purchase of books on international law, and also determined that the law collection in the Brynmor Jones Library be renamed 'The Sir Roy Marshall Law Library'. Philip observed: 'I can't help thinking there is something marsupial about putting the library of one Vice-Chancellor inside that of another.'

March 1985 marked the thirtieth anniversary of Philip's appointment as Librarian at Hull. It had been our wish to hold a celebration in the Brynmor Jones Library but Philip was already displaying symptoms of the illness that proved to be terminal and he did not feel equal to such an occasion. We postponed the plan, hoping that we could hold the affair when he was in better health but, of course, it was not to be. During April and May he was obviously unwell, clearly brooding over his symptoms and, after clinical investigations, he underwent surgery in June.

Dale Salwak and his wife were our house guests in late July, by which time Philip was home from hospital, although still weak, and he graciously consented to see the three of us. It was a Sunday afternoon and we had a pleasant visit culminating with my taking a photograph of Philip, Patti and Dale in front of the house since my flash attachment obstinately refused to function. It was the last photograph I took of Philip and it is reproduced as Plate 15 in this book.

Library problems soon surfaced after Philip's last Library Committee meeting. On 4 November interviews were scheduled for the appointment of a Deputy Librarian to succeed David Baker, who had recently become Librarian at the University of East Anglia. In the event Philip was not well enough to attend the

Selection Committee, no appointment was made and the post itself was subsequently eliminated as part of the University's financial savings. Philip was deeply concerned that the post of Deputy had not been filled and brooded over the implications for the library.

A presentation party was imminent for Maeve Brennan, to mark her early retirement after 32 years' service in the Brynmor Jones Library, at which both the Chairman of the Library Committee and the Librarian were to speak. It became apparent that, dearly as he would have liked to be there to pay tribute to his close friend and colleague of thirty years, it would not be possible. On 18 November Philip wrote to me about the function, concluding with the comment that 'I . . . generally feel very low indeed'. The following day he sent me the text of his tribute to Maeve and which I had agreed to read on his behalf. It was a poignant occasion.

That was the last communication I received from him. I telephoned his home a few days later to bring him up to date on library matters, only to learn that he had been readmitted to hospital; less than 48 hours later came the news that Philip had died.

For many months thereafter I experienced the sensation of entering a partial vacuum when I went into the Brynmor Jones Library; a vital spark was missing. Looking back over the period of our collaboration in library affairs, there is one memory that I especially cherish. The day following one particularly trying Library Committee our paths crossed by chance on the campus. After grumbling about the way things had gone at the meeting, Philip thanked me for presiding over a very difficult session and then added: 'But there are times you know, Eddie, when I do wish you would be rather less impartial', and his eyes twinkled.

Away from library affairs there are many happy recollections.

Soon after I had arrived in Hull *The Whitsun Weddings* was published and I asked Philip if he would inscribe my copy. This he duly did (only much later did I discover that I was among the favoured – not all of my colleagues were so honoured!), with an embellishment directed at my bookplate which, being designed to link my scientific and conjuring interests, depicts a bearded alchemist at work in his laboratory with a copy of John Baptista

Porta's *Natural Magic* (1658) on the bench – 'Not a bad likeness', penned Philip. Thereafter he was as intrigued by my conjuring activities as I was with his jazz proclivities, and over the succeeding years he took much delight in sending me news cuttings and notes about any aspects of conjuring that he came across in his extensive reading. Thus my files contain references provided by Philip to Edmund Wilson, Horace Spencer, Harry Price, among others, and include a poem by Frank Richards that appeared in *The Magnet* in 1932 concerning one Oliver Kipps, a Greyfriars boy whose hero was Jasper Maskelyne, the famous magician. Philip commented that he liked the stanza form although he suspected it was lifted from some well-known source, adding 'Gilbert and Sullivan unwittingly supplied a lot of his verse forms'. There is even an esoteric reference to the fact that one of Evelyn Waugh's sons went to a school 'kept by a conjuror named Dix', which turned out to be All Hallows, where F. H. R. Dix was headmaster and sometimes performed for the boys.

For New Year 1980 he sent me a cutting from the *Daily Telegraph* concerning a magician whose rabbit and £600-worth of props had been stolen from his car, and the admonition to 'Watch out'. Barely a week later it was followed by a 'Watch it No. 2', reporting substantial damage to a theatre by some rather inept magician who had managed to set fire to it. Some years earlier, having attended a show that I gave, Philip sent me a delightful note: 'I'd half hoped you would saw a professor in half, or double the library grant, but one mustn't expect too much.' As previously emphasised, the library grant always loomed large on Philip's horizon.

My friendship with Dale Salwak, the editor of this anthology, arose through our mutual interest in conjuring. It proved possible to arrange a dinner party with Philip on Dale's first visit with me in Hull (1982) and the evening was one which Philip, subsequently, was kind enough to refer to as one of the most remarkable he could recall. The occasion was magical in every sense for, after dinner, Dale changed into evening dress and performed his well-known sleight-of-hand act, complete with recorded accompaniment, for an audience comprising solely Philip, my wife and myself! Philip was happy, too, to participate in a three-person card trick, perhaps bearing in mind the inscription he had penned in my copy of *The Less Deceived*: 'To dear Eddie, reposing in his professorial chair (and performing the 3-card trick, probably) – these early lines.'

We had a standing joke about dinner which stemmed from an occasion when, at the conclusion of the meal, Philip opined that it was 'the most delicious chicken I have ever tasted', only to be informed by my wife that he had just consumed pheasant. Thereafter he took great delight in posing as a connoisseur of fowl.

Another friend with jazz interests is John Postgate, who was Director of the Agricultural and Food Research Council Unit of Nitrogen Fixation at the University of Sussex. He became a scientist when appendicitis robbed him of the opportunity to join Chris Barber's Jazz Band, after coming down from Oxford. John was not contemporary with Philip at Oxford but on the occasion of one of John's visits to Hull it was possible to stage manage a Jazz-Nitrogen Fixation Dinner when they met for the first time and discussed their jazz passions while I was an absorbed listener.

Philip enjoyed detective fiction and we shared an interest in the 'sealed room' style of murder mystery exemplified by the writings of John Dickson Carr, whose liking for magic and conjuring was not merely academic. When I secured a copy of *The Moving Toyshop* by Edmund Crispin (Bruce Montgomery), I was intrigued to see that it was dedicated to 'Philip Larkin in friendship and esteem', and Philip kindly told me the background to it. Although the story itself is set in Oxford, the plot takes as its starting point an observation that Philip actually made in Shrewsbury on one of his regular visits to see Bruce during the period of his (Philip's) first library post at Wellington (1945). On his scamper to catch the midnight train back he used to see one shop with its sunblind still down. Philip's report of it fascinated Bruce and thus it was incorporated into the story. My copy of the book carries Philip's inscription recording these circumstances.

Let me conclude these rambling recollections of Philip with a happy anecdote that concerns my Presidency of the Hull Literary & Philosophical Society during session 1976–7. It is the dubious privilege of the President to arrange the season's speakers and, bearing in mind the cliché that nowadays the Society is neither literary nor philosophical, I thought I should at least try to remedy the former deficiency. The Chairman of the Library Committee therefore endeavoured to 'pull rank' on the Secretary, Philip. I ought to have known better but the compensation was a charming letter declining my invitation, because he found the habits of a lifetime too strong. 'Some poets do enjoy reading to audiences, I know, and do it very well, but I should find it daunting and do it badly, if only that I've never done it in my life.' Philip went on to elaborate his fear that, if he relented, many long-refused bodies would leap on him again 'led by the Literary Club, whom I have stonewalled for 20 years'. The letter ended delightfully: 'I hate to say No to a friend, but when the only alternative is Yes, what can I do?' And as they say in showbusiness, 'You can't top that!'.

4

'I Remember, I Remember', 1955–85*

Maeve M. Brennan

When Miss Agnes Cuming, the retiring University Librarian, introduced us to her replacement, Philip Larkin, in March 1955, we wondered how this tall, spare, diffident young man would get on with us and we with him. By contrast, his dress was rather flamboyant: corduroy trousers, bright pink shirt and navy and white spotted bow tie. Later we were even more taken aback by the patterned ties with colourful fruit and flower designs which he alternated with the bow ties in those days, and his penchant for brightly coloured socks. Moreover, his intellectual appearance and pronounced stammer distanced him from us. We knew little about him except that he had come from Queen's University, Belfast, where he had been a sub-librarian, was thirty-two years old and unmarried. We knew nothing about his poetic aspirations and even the appearance of *The Less Deceived*, seven months after his arrival, caused no more than a faint ripple in our totally ordinary lives which were dominated by our boy friends, engagements and wedding plans, or their failure to come to fruition.

When Philip Larkin took over at Hull there were nine women on the staff and two men. Our average age was about twenty-one; only the Deputy Librarian was middle-aged. It did not seem possible that the newcomer's life and ours would ever touch – except remotely and then only in the course of our professional duties. But he quickly revealed a friendly nature and ready humour which drew him into our lives to an unexpected extent. Six months after his arrival, the younger of the two men on the staff was married, at mid-day in the middle of the working week. So that we could all (including Mr Larkin, as we then addressed

* I should like to thank David K. Bassett, Charles F. Brook, Brian Dyson, Frances Curnock-Newton, Anthony Thwaite and John White for their valuable comments.

him) attend the wedding ceremony, the Library was closed over lunch time, a unique occurrence in the Library's history. He made his own views on marriage known to us at an early stage. Nevertheless, he was intrigued by this young, mostly female staff he had inherited who, with the exception of one who was already married, were all either engaged or attached – a situation which caused a good deal of caustic comment on his part. Every Monday morning he would enquire mischievously: 'What's the news? Any more engagements? Or better still, have any been broken off? That's the sort of news I'd like to hear.' But we knew he was only teasing us and that fundamentally he wished us well in our (to his mind) misguided ways. We discovered soon enough that his sympathy was genuine when engagements were broken, as some were. He was also an astute judge of our partners. As he more than once remarked in such circumstances he 'could never understand how some of the nicest girls became involved with the most awful men'. Next time round he would make his views on the new partner equally clear so that his approval was something we came to value.

As a staff, because we were so small in number at this time, we were all very friendly, and our colleagues were often our closest friends. We saw a lot of each other outside working hours, and at times, especially at Christmas, someone would hold a party at home which we all attended, including the Librarian. By this time we openly called him 'Sir', an epithet we picked up from a book title, *To Sir, With Love*,[1] that caught his and our imagination. He was often somewhat at a loss in those early years in Hull: shy, at times very lonely, not a great socialiser, and consequently he felt most at ease with us. Without a car, he walked and cycled at the weekends all over what was then the East Riding. On Saturday afternoons (we worked in the mornings) he did his shopping, which he carried in a knapsack, and then invariably cycled to nearby Hessle where the Hartleys and the Marvell Press, responsible for publishing *The Less Deceived*, were to be found at the same address. For the first two or three years George and Jean Hartley were his closest local friends who, through their poetry magazine *Listen*,[2] were in touch with the contemporary literary scene in a way that no-one else in Hull was. Until the late 1960s, when the Hartleys separated, he was in constant touch with them – although they remained part of his circle for the rest of his life. At Christmas he, who was ill at ease with children, used to choose presents with great care for their two small daughters. He once gave them dolls. The thought of Philip actually going into a shop to buy dolls seemed incongruous but touching.

For the first eighteen months in Hull he lived in various digs or furnished accommodation where the lack of privacy greatly aggravated him. Contemplating some new-style round, aluminium pig styes which had recently been installed at a farm near one of his lodgings, he once wryly remarked: 'Those pigs have better accommodation than the Librarian of the University of Hull!' By the autumn of 1956, however, he was installed on the top floor of a tall Victorian house which was owned by the University and was situated on the edge of a small city park. The front windows opened on to tree tops, below which lay the park, tranquil and beautiful: the back windows looked on to roof tops and 'wedge-shadowed gardens'.[3] These are the High Windows which inspired the name of the title poem and the last collection. Across the main road from the park lie 'The Avenues', four long roads running from east to west, with large, attractive and distinctive houses built around the turn of the century. The crowning glory of this area, which still has a beauty untouched by urban development and vandalism, is the trees which line the wide verges of each avenue, forming a seasonal archway over the road of first pale, then dark green, and finally russet and gold. Philip loved these trees at all times of the year but especially in the autumn, when he took an almost child-like delight in walking through the thick carpet of fallen leaves. The trees and the scenes from those high windows come into many of his poems:

> I lose
> All but the outline of the still and withering
> Leaves on half-emptied trees . . .
> > ('Broadcast')

Apart from monthly weekend visits to his mother, Philip found Sundays particularly lonely in the early years at Hull. There was no companionship to be found in the University after the Library closed at 1 p.m. on Saturdays. On Sundays, therefore, he would sometimes ask one of us, if we happened to be free, to accompany him on cycle rides or walks. The open country is very accessible from Hull; in all directions one has only to travel three or four miles to reach wide, pleasant, if flattish, countryside. With

companions who did not cycle he would take a bus out of town
and plan a circular walk, or one which enabled them to pick up
the bus for the return journey further along the route. Sometimes
the walks would be local, exploring the Avenues' neighbourhood
or a nearby Victorian cemetery which held great fascination for
him. These outings usually ended with tea in the late afternoon at
a café, or sometimes at his flat or his companion's home. The
highlight for us was tea at his place where he invariably provided
toasted crumpets spread with Gentleman's Relish, and Earl Grey
tea, served in his primrose-decorated china tea service which was
brought out specially on these occasions. This was a very happy,
carefree era, enjoyed as much by Philip as by his companions;
there was an innocent charm and fun about it which was later lost
as life became more complex and sophisticated.

Life, of course, was not all play: there was much work to be
done. In 1955 Hull had only recently obtained University status,
having been affiliated to the University of London in its previous
twenty-six years. During this time the war had intervened, and
for a decade thereafter there was little money for expansion or
new buildings. However, an early priority was a purpose-built
Library, and on arrival Philip had to grapple with the architect's
plans which were already at an advanced stage and had to be
submitted to the University Grants Committee by December 1955.
It is always difficult to inherit someone else's ideas; for someone
of Philip's calibre it was impossible to accept them without
question. Therefore he set about modifying them, drawing heavily
on the theories assimilated during his Library Associateship
studies. This was one of the first post-war university libraries to
be built in the United Kingdom, so there was no established
model to draw on and little expert advice available. For long
periods Philip closeted himself in a hermit-like cell, far removed
from Library staff, readers and the telephone. This small hideout,
at the extremity of the top floor of the building in which the
Library was then accommodated, had large sloping shelves
designed for studying maps and bound volumes of newspapers.
There he spread out the plans for the new building and worked
on them most afternoons. We had strict instructions that his
whereabouts were not to be revealed nor was he to be interrupted
except on matters of urgency.

Building on the new site commenced in January 1958. Philip
watched the construction with all the pride and anxiety of a

mother for her first-born. During this period much week-end time was spent examining progress, photographing the shell of the building at various stages and noting features which displeased him. As the exterior neared completion and it became safe to enter, all the staff were taken over it, singly or in twos and threes, on Sundays. We regarded this as a great privilege and were as excited as our boss by the prospects of a purpose-built Library and a new working environment. When it was completed in August 1959, we were enchanted by the brightly coloured end-panels of the book stacks (colour denoted subject), the attractive tungsten lighting between each bay, the height, light, airiness and space of the catalogue hall and main reading room, the natural polished wood used for many of the fixtures, and the large oriel window, with seats round its base at the western end of the catalogue hall. We all participated in the move across the campus in the first seventeen days of September, sustained by a wonderful spirit of camaraderie and glorious weather. Half-way through the move Philip took us out to dinner at nearby Beverley, partly in celebration, partly in acknowledgement of the hard work we had so cheerfully undertaken. How else could we react when 'bliss was it in that dawn to be alive'?

Nine months after the new Library had opened to readers, it was officially opened by Her Majesty Queen Elizabeth, the Queen Mother, on a beautiful June day when the building was literally filled with flowers. As Philip himself recorded in his fifty-year history of the Library: 'This occasion was one of the happiest in the University's history.'[4] It was certainly a very splendid affair which took months of preparation. There was a magnificent lunch in the students' refectory (the largest dining room on the campus) for several hundred guests and staff, followed, after the official opening, by an equally lavish tea in the Library. Women at the lunch had to wear hats, long-sleeved dresses and gloves; in the afternoon the pretty hats of the Library staff were exchanged for mortar boards, and our colourful dresses were covered by drab academic gowns as we proudly showed visitors over the new building. The Queen Mother was, of course, looked after by the Chancellor, the Vice-Chancellor and the Librarian. Philip, for all his diffidence at this time, carried the day superbly, with justifiable pride and honour. We in turn felt very proud of him.

With Stage I of the building now completed, Philip turned his attention to other matters in the short interval before the plans for

Stage II began to occupy the greater part of his working time. The new environment stimulated his considerable flair for administration. He strengthened the Library Committee so that it became an influential sub-committee of the University Senate. His enterprising and well-defined acquisitions policies, which were generously supported by the Vice-Chancellor of that time, secured above-national-average funds for the Library. This, in due course, led to in-depth expansion of selected research interests, two such examples being twentieth-century English poetry, and emigration to the United States. The apparent ease with which Philip persuaded Senate to fund his projects, together with their implementation, brought considerable prestige to the Library.

He also began to take us to task more for our happy-go-lucky ways. He had a very sharp eye for anything out of place or untidy and never let any such thing pass without indicating his irritation. Once he allowed a glove and a bottle of nail varnish to remain on a shelf in the book sorting bay for 72 hours before his anger, tempered by mordant wit, broke on the unfortunate Library assistant who should have removed them as soon as they appeared. About 1960 he also decided to take his largely unqualified and unambitious staff in hand. Library Association examinations then were taken in one's own time in four parts. Assiduous non-graduate students usually took a year over each part; dedicated graduates aimed to complete them in a much shorter time. There were half a dozen of us, partially qualified, who had abandoned the struggle. We were all stuck at the most difficult section, cataloguing and classification, in spite of having attended classes at the City Library. Philip therefore undertook to give us tuition once or twice a week at lunch time over a period of some six months. He set us homework of typical examination questions which he marked with critical but helpful comments. Inevitably some fell by the wayside but those who persevered and succeeded gave him immense satisfaction. This was but one aspect of his solicitude for his staff. He always showed a particular concern for newcomers and, remembering his own unhappy experiences, never failed to enquire if they had satisfactory accommodation; if not, he gave them helpful advice. Likewise, he made a point of speaking to any member of staff whom he knew to be in personal difficulties, even when staff numbers increased to the point where it was no longer possible to be in close touch with everyone.

One luxury the new Library building included was a staff common room. Consequently, from 1959 onwards, Christmas parties were held in the Library instead of at individuals' homes. Since the whole building was at our disposal after closing time, there was greater scope for the presentation of party fare, dancing, competitions, films (two very funny films were made in the early 1960s by small teams of staff in which everyone featured, often unwittingly) and other entertainment. Whilst Philip later cultivated the image of a recluse, at this time he entered into the spirit of these unsophisticated parties with the same enthusiasm as the rest of us. One vivid recollection is of him emerging from the stack area behind the leader of a conga in which everyone had joined. In spite of his life-long passion for jazz and an innate sense of rhythm, he was not a natural dancer but could get by with shuffling to the music of the Beatles which then passed for dancing. Although their tunes held for him long afterwards a certain nostalgia, the insidious and liberating effect he felt the Beatles and similar groups had on the young and the not-so-young is accurately described in 'Annus Mirabilis':

> Sexual intercourse began
> In nineteen sixty-three
> (Which was rather late for me) –
> Between the end of the *Chatterley* ban
> And the Beatles' first LP.

In fact Philip's 'Annus Mirabilis' was 1964, when the year began with the publication of *The Whitsun Weddings* and later the same month (February) he bought his first car. The publication of *The Less Deceived* had marked him out as one of the leading poets of his generation; *The Whitsun Weddings* secured his place at the forefront of twentieth-century English poetry. Its immediate success prompted the BBC television documentary *Down Cemetery Road* which was filmed that summer and shown just before Christmas. 'Here' provided the location, with all the filming shot in and around Hull, showing the then bustling fish dock (now sadly defunct), the city centre, the derelict industrial wasteland on the banks of the River Hull, the wide windswept Humber estuary and the lonely emptiness of Holderness:

> Here is unfenced existence:
> Facing the sun, untalkative, out of reach.

The daily routines of Larkin, the Librarian, were also included, and although few of the staff appeared in the film, shots of most of us were taken going about our daily business. The Library's archives contain several interesting photographs of the television crew filming us! The making of the film amused and flattered Philip, but its showing made him very uneasy and he never again consented to appear on television even though the media caught him unawares on one or two subsequent occasions. He found their attention after Sir John Betjeman's memorial service in Westminster Abbey in August 1984 intrusive and offensive, and this was undoubtedly a major contributory factor in his unwillingness to be considered as the next Poet Laureate.

Meanwhile, Library expansion was by no means at a standstill. No sooner had we settled in our new and, by the standards of those days, luxurious environment than discussions for the next stage of building began to take place. By 1963 the architects had been engaged. They were a jolly partnership of four and for the next seven years the hard work of planning and compromise, followed by building and furnishing a much larger extension than Stage I, was enlivened by the close friendships struck up between client and architects. This time Philip involved all his senior colleagues in the planning of the new building to a degree undreamt of in our training days. The 1960s were a decade of rapid expansion in British universities and funds seemed to emanate from a bottomless pit. In this atmosphere we were all carried along on a wave of enthusiasm and excitement, and by 1970, when the refurbished Stage I had been most successfully integrated with Stage II, another pinnacle in Philip's career was reached. However, this did not give him the same fulfilment as the completion of Stage I had done a decade earlier and a period of disillusionment and fatigue set in. Nevertheless, much had been achieved since 1955, as Philip himself said with characteristic understatement in an interview in 1982: 'We built one new library in 1960 and another in 1970 so that my first fifteen years were busy.'[5]

Consequently, the invitation to spend the Michaelmas and Hilary terms of 1970–1 as a Visiting Fellow of All Souls College, Oxford, gave him a much-needed change. He wanted the time, and the facilities of the Bodleian Library, to complete the compilation of *The Oxford Book of Twentieth-Century English Verse* on which he had been working for several years. As a librarian of national stature and a poet of international renown, he was allowed to browse freely in areas of the Bodleian normally closed to readers. This greatly facilitated his research. Simultaneously, he enjoyed the intellectual companionship of fellow scholars at All Souls – where he had a small study and dined in the evenings – and lived in a College flat in parkland two or three miles from the centre of Oxford. He returned to Hull at intervals, being reluctant to let go of the reins completely. On one surprise visit, whilst grudgingly accepting that the assistants on the issue desk had taken advantage of his absence to exchange skirts for slacks, which had not previously been permitted, he commented with that inimitable wry humour that he was relieved not to find too many bottles about! Of course there were none; it was simply his way of admitting that all was running surprisingly smoothly.

His fiftieth birthday in 1972 was a great watershed in his life and one which he was convinced would signal the decline of his creative ability. This belief persisted in spite of his having been widely tipped to succeed Cecil Day-Lewis as Poet Laureate that year, the controversial success of *The Oxford Book of Twentieth-Century English Verse* in 1973 (some reviewers were critical of his choices) and the immediate success of *High Windows* in 1974 when he was hailed the undisputed leading poet of the day. The public acclaim only seemed to accentuate his inner depression. By now, he saw himself increasingly as the reluctant party guest portrayed in 'Vers de Société':

> Holding a glass of washing sherry, canted
> Over to catch the drivel of some bitch
> Who's read nothing but *Which*;

but ever-mindful that

> The time is shorter now for company

and being alone no longer brings contentment but the fear of approaching age 'and then the only end of age'.[6]

His domestic circumstances were also changing and left him less time for creative writing. Weekends were increasingly spent visiting his mother, already past her mid-eighties, who was living some hundred miles distant in the south-east Midlands. In 1974, after eighteen years there, he left the University flat with the high windows for a modest house with a large garden which absorbed still more of his time. This move was traumatic, not only in that it changed his lifestyle, but also because he never enjoyed in the new house the tranquillity and inspiration he had found in the flat where he had spent the happiest and most creatively successful period of his life. There he had written his two most popular collections of verse, had enjoyed for ten years writing the weekly jazz reviews for the *Daily Telegraph* and reviewed numerous books. Simultaneously, the two library buildings, each so largely his brainchild, had been built and their shelves judiciously filled. There was little wonder he doubted that he would ever again achieve so much.

Sadly, in the remaining eleven years of his life, he fretted greatly about the Muse's desertion which he had foreseen, and increasingly the spectre of death haunted him. This fear is vividly set down in his last great poem, 'Aubade', which was first published in *The Times Literary Supplement* in December 1977. The terror and bleakness of death, the denial of any Christian consolation, the appalling fear of annihilation which he saw as the end of life, are described in uncompromisingly bleak terms:

> the total emptiness forever,
> The sure extinction that we travel to
> And shall be lost in always.

The last decade was not all gloom, however. Philip's power of mimicry and tremendous sense of humour continued to sustain him and amuse friends and colleagues. At the last staff retirement party at which he presided, less than two months before his death, his wit was both at its sharpest and most affectionate. Gently highlighting the foibles of the retiree, he described how she had been appointed for three years, seventeen years earlier, to organise an admittedly large and messy collection of labour history material which, in 1985, still remained 'a wasteland of seditious literature'. He still frequented social gatherings but with less zest than formerly: in addition, acute deafness intensified his difficulties on social and formal occasions. At home he saw only close friends over a drink, the delightful teas of crumpets and Gentleman's Relish were but memories of the happier past. One nostalgic ritual he kept up almost to the end, however, was the celebration of Hallowe'en when he made mulled wine and hung up the little models of witches on broomsticks he had had for years.

Throughout the 1970s Philip had been cautious about the introduction of automation into the Library but in 1980 a highly sophisticated Canadian system, specialising in library functions, was installed. Courageously Philip was the first librarian in Europe to adopt the system. Its installation gave a much-needed stimulus to the Library, which had recently been affected by financial cutbacks, so that once more, as in 1960 and 1970, Philip took pride in the fact that the Library again became a focus of national attention and envy.

In the last year his decline was rapid. At Christmas 1984 he expressed deep unease about his health. In the New Year, urged by close friends, he reluctantly sought medical advice. By June a serious condition had been diagnosed, necessitating immediate surgery. This gave him all too short a remission and from late autumn he deteriorated quickly. For his friends, one of their saddest realisations was that in those last months he experienced with such painful intensity the fears so vividly expressed in 'Aubade'; this anguish no one could assuage. With committed Christians Philip would argue that he did not have the consolation which religion gave them in the face of death. And yet he envied those who had faith, and fervently wished he too could embrace it. His funeral service in the church of St Mary the Virgin, Cottingham, on 9 December 1985, which was conducted in the best Anglican tradition was, one felt, in spite of his incapacity to believe, as he would have wanted it and therefore wholly appropriate. In one sense the annihilation he dreaded – 'nothing contravenes/The coming dark'[7] – was unfounded, for Philip Larkin's poetry will almost certainly continue to be read long after other poets of his generation have been forgotten.

> Nor shall death brag thou wander'st in his shade,
> When in eternal lines to time thou grow'st
> So long as men can breathe, or eyes can see,
> So long lives this, and this gives life to thee.[8]

5

'Goodbye, Witherspoon': a Jazz Friendship

John White

Sometime in January 1965, during my first week as an assistant lecturer in American Studies at the University of Hull, I wandered into the refectory bar and overheard two men discussing the composition of various jazz rhythm sections. I recognised one of the talkers as an eminent professor of history; the other – balding, bespectacled, 'death-suited' – I guessed might be Philip Larkin. Before arriving in Hull, I had read *The Whitsun Weddings*, and the poems 'Reference Back' and 'For Sidney Bechet' had struck responsive chords, particularly the lines about 'scholars *manqués* . . . Wrapped up in personnels like old plaids'. When I heard the professor's drinking companion ask: 'And who was that farting about on the drums?', I knew that my surmise had been correct. Too awed to introduce myself, I retreated to the bookstore and purchased a copy of *The Less Deceived*. The next day, I spotted Philip alone at the bar, assumed that he recognised me as an academic, and remarked (for want of anything less fatuous to say) that there had been remarkably few students present at my just-finished lecture. Eyeing me suspiciously, he replied: 'Well, they don't want old fogeys like me, and they don't want smart alecks like you.' The first words spoken to me by Philip Larkin, I decided, constituted a black eye, rather than a feather in my cap. Twenty years later, I reminded him jokingly of the episode. Mortified, in retrospect, at this seeming lapse from his generally unfailing courtesy – even to supercilious assistant lecturers – he protested and apologised in a letter: 'Please forget the smart aleck business – it was years ago, and a v. thoughtless thing of me to say. I shouldn't dream of saying it now.' He also invited me to join a newly formed university Dining Club that was 'all right, but lonely and ladylike. Not enough drinkers'.[1]

Following the inauspicious old fogey/smart aleck incident,

through chance encounters and at assorted functions, I came to
regard Philip first as a colleague, and then as a friend. From time
to time, he would send me queries about Americanisms he had
encountered. The first, I remember, concerning the etymology of
'Canned Heat' (the name of a current pop group), and we also
began to talk about our mutual love of jazz – although not always
the same kinds of jazz. Philip's jazz heroes and heroines, as I
quickly discovered, were a select band – King Oliver, Duke
Ellington, Sidney Bechet, Pee Wee Russell. My own jazz tastes
are more eclectic, or, as he informed me loudly and lugubriously
on one occasion in the Brynmor Jones Library (and to the alarm
of passing students): 'You are one of those buggers who likes
everybody.'

He expressed a similar complaint, more elegantly, in a review
(not widely known) for *The American Scholar*, of *New Yorker* critic
Whitney Balliett's collected essays on jazz, *Night Creature*:

> a critic, after all, is a man who likes some things and dislikes
> others, and finds reasons for doing so and for trying to persuade
> other people to do so. This is altogether alien to Balliett's
> purposes. Balliett, in short, recalls Arnold Bennett's impatient
> comment: 'Hang Eddie Marsh! He's a miserable fellow – he
> enjoys everything.'[2]

Unlike Eddie Marsh or Whitney Balliett, Philip did not enjoy
everything in (or that passed for) jazz. If he would not have hung
the likes of Sonny Rollins, Archie Shepp, Albert Ayler and Miles
Davis, he certainly did not wish them well. But Philip's admiration
(which we shared) for Balliett as a prose stylist was real, and
received, in the same review, glowing commendation:

> He writes in the first-night tradition of Kenneth Tynan and A. J.
> Liebling, in which what is said arises from a particular occasion
> and is designed in part to eternalise it. . . . Balliett's writing is
> instinctively pictorial: simile and metaphor, adjective and adverb
> all cohere and jump to tell us *what it was like to be there.* . . .
> every so often he unites these talents in a larger tapestry. He
> will visit a player, tape what he says, and carefully interweave
> large stretches of this vernacular with his own studied narrative
> to several thousand words' length, achieving what in the trade
> is called a profile but is really a Van Dyck portrait. . . . The

achievement is the more remarkable by reason of the gentle courtesy with which it is done. The fascination of a Balliett collection lies in watching his hypersensitive technique (a combination of Leica and lapel mike) receive and transmit so many various musical experiences.[3]

In his own (and equally inimitable) way, of course, Philip could convey to his readers (and to his listeners) the joys and tribulations of the music he had first discovered in 'adolescence between the wars'. Philip's definition of the real jazz was memorably expressed in 'Credo' (1967):

> A. E. Housman said he could recognise poetry because it made his throat tighten and his eyes water: I can recognise jazz because it makes me tap my foot, grunt affirmative exhortations, or even get up and caper 'round the room. If it doesn't do this, then however musically interesting or spiritually adventurous or racially praiseworthy it is, it isn't jazz.[4]

I count myself as one of those fortunate enough to have seen Philip practise what he so fervently preached. At some point during our (widely-spaced) evenings of listening to jazz records, sometimes in the company of one or two like-minded friends, Philip – pleasantly replete with the whisky he always thoughtfully provided – would rise from his chair, grin happily, and execute a few ponderous dance steps to the strains of Earl Bostic's exhilaratingly vulgar rendition of 'Flamingo' or Eddie Condon's extended version of 'How Come You Do Me Like You Do'. In later years, as he became progressively deafer, whistling noises from Philip's hearing aid accompanied our record recitals. Since he declined, after one eyeball-rolling demonstration, to make use of stereophonic headphones, the solution was simply to turn up the volume at the risk of arousing neighbours.

Record evenings with Philip followed a comfortably familiar pattern: academic gossip (with Philip expressing himself in what used to be called 'colourful language'); obligatory genuflections to Eddie Condon, Benny Goodman, Duke Ellington and vintage Count Basie. Then we would bring out the great blues shouters – Jimmy Witherspoon, Joe Turner, Jimmy Rushing. Witherspoon was our Main Man. In many of his well-worn blues – usually about advancing age and/or the loss of his woman Witherspoon interjects a personal note, viz.: 'When I went to see my baby, she pulled the shades and locked the door/She said goodbye, Witherspoon, I can't use your rollin' no more.' Repeated playings of such lyrics elicited from Philip the thought that the events recounted by 'Spoon always reminded him of one of those King and Country films of the 1940s, in which the hero receives a handshake from his superior at the Foreign Office, and the ritual farewell: 'Goodbye, Witherspoon, it takes a brave man to go where you're going', etc.

It was one of Philip's gifts to perceive and reveal humour in unlikely situations – at the same time, leaving one in no doubt as to his real feelings in the matter. Addressing the Hull Jazz Record Society (an organisation which he preferred to support in spirit, rather than in the flesh), Philip discoursed amusingly on 'My Life and Death as a Record Reviewer'. After playing a characteristically jagged and fumbling piano solo by Thelonious Monk (generally acknowledged as one of the giants of modern jazz), he suggested mischievously that listening to Monk was like walking down a street, passing an open window and hearing someone's sister practising scales – an analogy that startled, if it did not convince, most of his audience. In addition to records which had received the Larkin seal of approval – by the Chicago Rhythm Kings, Red Nichols, Art Hodes and Billy Banks (one of Philip's most cherished records) – he also 'inflicted' liberal doses of his *bêtes noires* – Miles Davis, Albert Ayler, John Coltrane and Charlie Parker – on assembled jazz *afficionados* considerably further left than Philip was to the right in their tastes.

Philip was well aware that his opinions on modern jazz – and his views on modernism in the arts in general 'whether perpetrated by Parker, Pound or Picasso' – met with disbelief, derision, scorn and condemnation within the jazz (and near-jazz) fraternity on both sides of the Atlantic. In 1984, when I was teaching at a black college in Alabama, he wrote:

A new edition of *All What Jazz* is coming out soon but I'll save your copy for you. In fact it should be out in the USA about the same time, so better keep quiet that you know me. It now reads very anti-black, insofar as most of the people I ballock are black. Coltrane, Coleman, Shepp. But then most of the people I praise are black too. Better play safe.[5]

He was very pleased when I sent him American reviews of the book. One, from the British-born critic Stanley Dance, elicited the response: 'No Laureateship – thanks for the Dance.' And, in another letter: 'Thank you for the Dance review – jolly nice and sympathetic. I could tell he agreed with every word I said, but daren't say so.' (The same letter, written in November 1984, also contained a request, an explanation and an expletive. 'Buy me a raccoon coat, will you, to wear *indoors* this winter. The Estates Office is already living up to its motto "Heating People is Wrong"; "We don't issue supplementary heaters when the main heating isn't on." Jesus.')[6] Another communication contained Philip's succinct reactions to Terry Southern's scurrilous novel, *Blue Movie*, which I had passed on to him before I left England: 'Somewhat disgusting, somewhat arousing, more funny than anything else. I liked the electrician doing a nose-dive from the upper gantries on the set.'[7]

My copy of the first edition of *All What Jazz* (1970) is inscribed: 'All best for John, from his illiterate (jazzwise) foot-stomping colleague, Philip.' The inscription thirteen years later in *Required Writing* (1983), reads simply: 'from "Slow Drag" Larkin'. Between these seminal dates, I came to understand more clearly and to benefit tangibly from Philip's love of jazz. A request to borrow a record from his collection (with a convenient check-list provided in *All What Jazz*) saw Philip pull out his pocket-handkerchief, and solemnly tie a large knot. The desired album was usually available for collection at his office the next day.

A plea of mine for a record he had reviewed with faint praise for the *Daily Telegraph* – ' "Stitt Plays Bird" . . . might have done better in a month that didn't include "Charlie Parker – Historical Masterpieces". . . . Sonny turns in nine Parker standards pleasantly enough, but his tone lacks that free cutting edge that gave Bird wings' – produced an unexpected and delightfully incongruous response: 'No sign of "Stitt Plays Bird", I'm afraid. Would you have any use for this [Edmund]Wilson Symposium? It has a few interesting things in it.'[8] On another occasion, I was the grateful recipient of Philip's duplicate copies of four Bessie Smith LPs and, in the same parcel, seven albums by the tenor saxophonist Sonny Rollins. Checking in *All What Jazz*, I discovered a faintly disturbing explanation for Philip's generosity regarding Rollins:

Since his two-year retirement . . . Rollins as his present records demonstrate, has been thrashing around chaotically, producing sounds of such repellent harshness that the listener feels he is being pelted with slivers of granite. Not that he was ever noted for mellifluity. . . . Listening to him was brutally stimulating, like a Finnish *sauna*. His solos were like iron, like untreated concrete, full of anger and non serviam. . . . How far his present Ornette-derived manner, like his Mohican haircut and Zen allegiances, is part of a consciously-adopted *persona* is uncertain.[9]

In the case of Bessie Smith, Philip had offered due recognition tempered by astute qualification:

Some of her records . . . are beautiful in a way nothing else in jazz equals. But the change of taste that abandoned Bessie as a primitive could see what we prefer to ignore: that her voice was sometimes merely harsh and loud, that she could be monotonously repetitive, that her accompaniment could be grotesquely facetious. . . . This collection . . . commemorates a unique and imperious talent which at its best commanded a sombre tragedy as rare as it is moving.[10]

Once, Philip was acutely embarrassed to have placed himself in the position of Indian-giver. A short note explained (and resolved) his dilemma: 'I blush to admit it, but the [Earl] Hines record I gave you *wasn't* a duplicate. So can I have it back? This one – "Swinging in Chicago" – *is*, and you are welcome to it.' Reading Philip's review of the record, I wondered if there was a note of irony in his *largesse*:

The Hines group, 'Swinging in Chicago', is the Grand Terrace Orchestra, harsh, heavy and – except for Hines – somewhat archaic, like a gangster's sedan. . . . Hines's piano touch is like the kick of a mule. As a jazz performer he is astonishing, possessing right from his early twenties a completely original style (like Bechet and Armstrong), yet (to my mind at least) always producing music that is a little inhuman, a little comfortless, a Merlin of the Keyboard one can admire but not cherish.[11]

In return for Philip's munificence, I provided him with books, records and tapes from my own library – loans which were invariably returned with an appreciative message. On a visit to New York City, I went to Eddie Condon's jazz club (it had retained the name after his death), on West 54th Street and on my return to Hull gave Philip two souvenirs of the pilgrimage – a copy of the drinks menu and a book of matches, both emblazoned with the legend 'Eddie Condon's'. For these ephemera, I received a handwritten note that only Philip could have composed: 'Thanks for bits of the true Condon cross. PAL.' But I have no recollection of what prompted the following: 'Many thanks for lending me this. Paris sides a thought ponderous, but all v. good listening.'

Over the years, the exchanges of jazz materials continued. Since Philip – as much from self-confessed consumer laziness as from principle ('If I were to frame Larkin's Law of Reissues, it would say that anything you haven't got already probably isn't worth bothering about') – bought very few new records, I was able to provide him with some notable issues (and reissues) he had not heard.[12] I once gave him simple and specific instructions of how to get to a jazz-specialising record shop a few strides from King's Cross Station, on Gray's Inn Road. When I asked him, after a London trip, if he had paid it a visit, he replied sheepishly that he had been unable to locate the premises, had panicked and ended up in an amusement arcade – an explanation which I was not expected to find entirely plausible. And it was only with considerable difficulty that Philip could be persuaded to attend live jazz performances, as thin as they are on the ground in Hull – 'Where only salesmen and relations come'.[13] He did, however, consent to go to a few such events on the campus – most memorably, a Duke Ellington Memorial Concert in May 1984, which featured the veteran black singer, Adelaide Hall. Philip, accompanied by Monica Jones, was seen to be visibly enjoying the proceedings – towards the staging of which he had made a generous (but anonymous) financial contribution. An earlier visit by two accomplished American performers – Bob Wilber and Kenny Davern – also drew appreciative noises and much foot-stomping from a delighted Philip.

One jazz evening spent at Philip's house (there were just the two of us) stands out in my memory. He had obviously gone to some trouble – in addition to the mandatory beer and whisky, there were also sandwiches, cakes and coffee. The session, I felt, was going very happily: Philip's preferred jazzmen blasting from the hi-fi, shared responses to felicitous phrases, casual, jazz-centred conversation, browsings through his impressive record collection. Quite suddenly, and, I felt, *à propos* of nothing that had gone before, he asked me if I had ever thought of transposing the decades of a human life into days of the week. I confessed that I had not. Philip, not surprisingly, had, and informed me grimly that he was 'on' Friday afternoon. With forced cheerfulness, I replied that I hoped I was only somewhere near Wednesday morning, but he didn't seem to register the remark. Then he said with decisive conviction: 'Sometimes, I think the only thing to do is just to sell up everything and wait for the knock on the door.' The mood lifted as suddenly as it had appeared. My recollection of the remainder of the evening is of roughly equal proportions of jazz and Scotch, and Philip's intriguing explanation of the hidden meaning of the words 'porters larking with the mails' in 'The Whitsun Weddings'. When I said that Larkinophiles at the University of Texas would pay handsomely for such classified information, he said expansively: 'Take it, dear boy.'

In one of his record reviews 'Make Me a Palate', Philip wrote:

Back from a holiday where the only music came from waiters' beach radios, my scoured palate revels in the accumulation of recent records. While an exciting multi-layered sandwich works slowly down the spindle of my record-player, I realise afresh the truth of Baudelaire's words: 'Man can live a week without bread, but not a day without the righteous jazz.'[14]

But, as I discovered when visiting him in hospital during what was to prove his final illness, Philip, obsessed with thoughts of death, had, for a time at least, rejected 'Baudelaire's' dictum. He refused the offer of jazz cassettes to play in his room, and was doubtful whether he would want to listen to records when (and if) he returned home. I assured him that his need for jazz would return and, for a brief time after his discharge from hospital, it seemed to. I saw him in the university bar, seemingly much better, and certainly willing to talk about the recent demise of several noted jazz players. I gave him a cassette recording of a radio programme celebrating the work of two jazz drummers, Jo Jones and Philly Joe Jones, who had died in the same week – the first, a Larkin favourite, the second, a member of the 'modernist'

jazz school which he sometimes pretended to like for the benefit
of *Daily Telegraph* readers. He promised to listen to both tributes,
and possibly did, but went back into hospital for the last time
before I was able to ask for his verdicts.

Jazz Journal International – a magazine to which Philip regularly
subscribed – carried a notice of his death by the critic Steve Voce.
He was, Voce asserted:

> our greatest poet and a man who wrote on the subject of jazz
> with great sensitivity, although he constantly belittled himself
> without cause. He was a far more perceptive listener than I,
> and I was embarrassed when he wrote to me as recently as
> September [1985] 'You really mustn't think of me as someone in
> your league jazzwise . . .'. What nonsense! He loved *Jazz Journal*
> *International* and claimed to 'take a certain unregenerate pleasure
> in the protests you sometimes evoke with your column.'[15]

Philip had been 'overjoyed', Voce revealed, when the visiting
American trumpeter Buck Clayton had included the message 'I'm
enjoying the book' (the revised edition of *All What Jazz*) in one of
his letters.[16] (Philip had once described Clayton as 'an excellent
player but rather clean-limbed for my taste'.) Philip's jazz
friendships cast a wide net. He corresponded with many fellow
enthusiasts – including Alistair Cooke – who endorsed his maxim
that 'a critic is only as good as his ear'. But in Philip's case, the
critic was also as good as his superlative pen. Whitney Balliett
would surely applaud the vivid description of Sidney Bechet's
'Blue Horizon';

> six choruses of slow blues in which Bechet climbs without
> interruption or hurry from lower to upper register, his clarinet
> tone at first thick and throbbing, then soaring like Melba in an
> extraordinary blend of lyricism and power that constituted the
> unique Bechet voice, commanding attention the instant it
> sounded.[17]

A distinguished jazz ensemble played at Philip's Memorial
Service in Westminster Abbey on 14 February 1986. The moving
recreations of his favourite tunes – 'Blue Horizon' (Bechet),
'Davenport Blues' (Beiderbecke) and trumpeter Alan Elsdon's
plangent solo performance of 'A Closer Walk With Thee' –

impressed the large congregation of friends and admirers. Of all the many tributes to his life and work, these were the most fitting and sadly appropriate – and surely more to Philip's liking than the prayers and recitations of his poems up at the 'holy end' of the Abbey. I thought of 'Goodbye, Witherspoon', and the closing lines of 'For Sidney Bechet':

> On me your voice falls as they say love should,
> Like an enormous yes. My Crescent City
> Is where your speech alone is understood,
>
> And greeted as the natural noise of good,
> Scattering long-haired grief and scored pity.

6

Philip Larkin Abroad

Janice Rossen

A fascinating aspect of Larkin's poetic treatment of England is his attitude towards what is not England: that is, Abroad. This vast uncharted territory strikes terror into his heart, or so he confesses to be the case: 'I hate being abroad', he declared in an interview. 'Generally speaking, the further one gets from home the greater the misery.'[1] His manifest hatred of what was 'not home' took various and increasingly humorous forms. Letters and postcards to friends while on holiday (invariably in the British Isles) bear occasional resentful and witty exhortations to eschew travel. Letters to novelist Barbara Pym occasionally find Larkin furious at his hotel. He waxes eloquent on the subject of appalling food and accommodation: 'why are single rooms *so much worse* than double ones? Fewer, further, frowstier? Damper, darker, dingier? Noisier, narrower, nastier?'[2] At times he despairs of holidays in general, which comprise a modern counterpart of medieval pilgrimages in that they are 'essentially a kind of penance for being so happy and comfortable in one's daily life'.[3]

This exaggerated fear of travel expresses from an oblique angle Larkin's habitual sense of alienation and isolation. Numerous influences confirm his unshakable prejudice against leaving British shores. Still another letter to Pym finds Larkin having hardened in his resolve to stay near home. In 1963 he wrote to her that Kingsley Amis's latest novel (*One Fat Englishman*) 'takes its place among all the other books that don't make me want to visit America'.[4] He resolutely declined invitations to visit or to lecture at universities in the States. Another letter to Pym finds him suspicious of a latest offer to participate in a professional gathering in Washington, DC, where he hazards that the academics involved probably 'spend time "leading discussions" and "contributing to seminars"'. Such an idea was vehemently declared to be unwelcome: 'Over my head. Over my dead body.'[5]

He seemed to relish warnings against undertaking such a trip.

On one occasion I was privileged to meet Professor Larkin; he paid tribute to my nationality by relating a story about crime in New York City. Apparently a friend of his, while on a visit to the States, had determined to consult the New York Public Library on a Sunday afternoon. On the way up the steps to the door, he was accosted by 'three unreliable characters', who asked for money. The friend indignantly refused. Upon reaching the door, he found that the library was closed on the afternoon in question. Unfortunately, his return down the same steps resulted in a reappearance of the same 'three unreliable characters' who promptly mugged him in return for his earlier churlishness. This incident, occurring *'on the steps of a library'*, Larkin emphasised, had been the absolute deciding factor in his refusal to visit the States.

An elaborate fantasy of painless travel broadens in his remark in an interview, where he admitted: 'I wouldn't mind seeing China if I could come back the same day.'[6] He was, in fact, persuaded to travel to Hamburg, Germany, in 1976 in order to accept the Shakespeare Prize confirmed on him by the city. To refuse to attend the ceremony would have been discourteous, and Larkin was an eminently gracious man. The prospect of the journey and festivities seemed to Larkin at the time to be 'VERY FAR from all very well', as he wrote in a letter to Sir John Betjeman.[7] The resulting trip could not be suffered to pass without a redeeming joke. In a copy of the programme for the presentation ceremony, which Larkin gave to his friend Professor Garnet Rees (Professor of French at the University of Hull) and Mrs Rees, Larkin inscribed the inside cover: 'To Garnet and Dilys, from Philip "Marco Polo" Larkin'.

Not all of his venom is reserved for travel 'Abroad' – attendance at librarianship conferences in England often produced moans and complaints about inadequate comforts while staying away from home. Larkin agreed most vigorously with Barbara Pym about the crucial importance of a proper reading light next to the bed. On the occasion of a visit to All Souls, Larkin declared in a letter to her: 'Oxford luxury is a myth. No shade on the guest room lamp!'[8] Even a place as familiar to him as Oxford could cause anxiety. He wrote to Pym describing a recent visit: 'Oxford was its usual self: heavenly for 24 hours, then I couldn't get away fast enough. It's always the same.'[9]

Apart from the question of holidays, Larkin's decision to stay in Hull for thirty years seems part of this general value for comfort and familiarity. 'Hull is a place where I *have* stayed', was his tart answer to a long and involved question from an interviewer about Larkin's place of residence, and his relation to the poet in 'Places, Loved Ones'. He went on to describe an anniversary luncheon at the Brynmor Jones Library on the occasion of his twenty-fifth anniversary there, in which staff members 'made me a presentation with a card bearing the very lines you mean. *Touché*, as the French say.'[10] His prolonged stay in Hull provided a source of private amusement, as other comments made in interviews suggest; Larkin felt safely isolated on the 'periphery' of England.

> I love all the Americans getting on to the train at King's Cross and thinking they're going to come and bother me, and then looking at the connections and deciding they'll go to Newcastle and bother Basil Bunting instead. Makes it harder for people to get at you.[11]

These comments suggest the beneficial effects of isolation; to be alone is to be secure and thus protected from intrusion. Larkin relished the description of Hull as being 'on the way to nowhere', and approved of its being in the middle of a 'lonely country'.[12] His poem about Hull entitled 'Here' emphasises this aspect from its opening lines:

> Swerving east, from rich industrial shadows
> And traffic all night north; swerving through fields
> Too thin and thistled to be called meadows,
> And now and then a harsh-named halt, that
>   shields
> Workmen at dawn; swerving to solitude . . .

Hull becomes a kind of sanctuary which provides solitude. The 'here' of the title actually becomes displaced to the uninhabited area outside the city: 'Here silence stands/Like heat. Here leaves unnoticed thicken', and finally, 'Here is unfenced existence'. Even in England, Hull and its environs become a refuge within the larger, insulated island of England.

Within this framework of the town one inhabits, Larkin also assigned great importance to one's particular dwelling. The poem 'Mr Bleaney' directly equates the poet's hired room with his worth as a man: 'how we live measures our own nature'. On a less sombre note, Larkin consistently showed concern in such matters for his staff at Brynmor Jones Library. In his position as University Librarian, he assumed that 'lodgings' were of immense importance to others as well. He always inquired of newly arrived staff if they had found 'suitable accommodation'.[13] He seemed acutely sensitive to his own lodgings, changing rooms five or six times during his first few years in Hull. Even his relatively comfortable flat at Pearson Park gave occasional cause for complaint. A letter to Pym finds Larkin decrying the disturbance made by banging doors in the flat below – noise made, he hazards, by people who are either 'perpetually quarrelling' or who are possibly 'new to houses with doors'. He concludes in mock despair that he might after all be more comfortable in a bungalow: 'There must be *some* limit to the things money can't buy.'[14]

Isolation, in Larkin's view, can be helpful as a defence against the world. But travel – even within the relatively safe and well-known confines of England – can produce alienation of an unpleasant sort. The consciousness of aloneness and futility which Larkin's protagonist feels in 'Dockery and Son' is first made palpable by his solitary departure from Oxford: 'I catch my train, ignored./Canal and clouds and colleges subside/Slowly from view.'

Much of Larkin's descriptive poetry about England itself is written from the point of a detached observer. He shows a continual tendency to consider what the country might look like to a tourist – foreign or otherwise – and envisions with concern the possibility that decaying England might be preserved only to be locked into museums and galleries. In 'Church Going', the poet meditates on the fate of redundant churches, wondering 'if we shall keep/A few cathedrals chronically on show,/Their parchment, plate and pyx in locked cases'. Similarly, in 'Going, Going' the poet envisions England's survival at one remove: 'There'll be books; it will linger on/In galleries; but all that remains/For us will be concrete and tyres'. The protagonist himself often observed social rituals from the point of view of a detached spectator, as in 'Show Saturday', 'To the Sea', and 'The Whitsun Weddings'. In these poems the speaker uses his position as a detached observer in order to discern the universal, recurring elements which lie beneath social rituals. The seaside holidaying in 'To the Sea' comforts because of its repetition of former occasions: 'Still going on, all of it, still going on!' Similarly, the yearly gathering in 'Show Saturday' comprises 'Regenerate union'.

In the way that Hull offers a beneficial protective isolation to the poet, these social events provide a stage for detached observations about ordinary yet significant events. Andrew Motion firmly places Larkin in a long line of 'intensely patriotic' yet 'unjingoistic' poets such as Wordsworth, Tennyson, Hardy, Edward Thomas, A. E. Housman and Auden, all of whom are 'centrally concerned with the relationship between themselves and their towns or landscapes, and habitually express a sense of communion with their surroundings in exalted or even semi-mystical terms'.[15] England itself is Larkin's primary subject, as he affirms by stating that travel is necessary for a novelist, who requires new material for his fiction, but not for a poet: 'The poet is really engaged in recreating the familiar, he's not committed to introducing the unfamiliar.'[16]

At the same time, the concept of Abroad fills a particular role in Larkin's work. His satirisation of Abroad – often masked as mockery of self – constitutes a private revenge on the horrors of the outside world in general. It also helps to define his position in relation to England. 'The Importance of Elsewhere' illustrates the role of Larkin's ambivalence toward England itself in terms of being the English tourist abroad. It reverses the poet's habitual sense of isolation from his surroundings to work instead to his advantage:

> Lonely in Ireland, since it was not home,
> Strangeness made sense. The salt rebuff of speech,
> Insisting so on difference, made me welcome:
> Once that was recognised, we were in touch.

He remains isolated or 'lonely', but since he is abroad (though in the British Isles, of course) this alienation seems expected and accepted. It makes 'sense', and further creates an abrasive sense of connection. Transferred back to England, though, the same phenomenon of isolation turns against him:

> Living in England has no such excuse:
> These are my customs and establishments
> It would be much more serious to refuse.
> Here no elsewhere underwrites my existence.

Possessing an identity or home which is displaced elsewhere provides security – one can always fall back on the existence of an alternative identity, and thus avoid the unpleasant reality of the present place and time. Larkin seems to have engineered his own exchange by creating and embellishing a myth of Abroad; the more exotic that 'abroad' (or a foreign 'elsewhere') seems, the more homely and familiar home becomes in contrast. Larkin carries the myth of insularity to an extreme as a paradigm for the larger loneliness and depression he experienced. He transforms this disconnection and detachment from England into a close yet dispassionate study of its monuments, its social festivals and its unregarded trash littering the countryside. As an observer, and not as a participant, he seems to have felt most at home, and most thoroughly English.

7

An Innocent at Home

Noel Hughes

Nothing about Philip Larkin has proved quite so lastingly baffling as his attitude to 'abroad' and to the people who live there. Larkin himself seemed to pose the conundrum with fierce aggression. Asked of Jorge Luis Borges, he countered with: 'Who's Jorge Luis Borges?' To the suggestion that he might, with advantage, read Laforgue, he replied: 'If that chap Laforgue wants me to read him he'd better start writing in English.' And to the proposition that he might care to visit China his answer was: 'I wouldn't mind seeing China if I could come back the same day.'[1]

An obvious explanation is that he was an ill-bred, narrow-minded cretin; but it won't do because he was none of these things. Larkin offered a rare explanation in an interview with Miriam Gross. He told her of his visits to Germany, as a teenager, with his parents: 'I think this sowed the seed of my hatred of abroad – not being able to talk to anyone or read anything'.[2] It was an astute remark. You could hardly be responsible – and so called on to justify – an attitude imbibed, if not quite with mother's milk, then at least with the nursery jelly. The trouble with this explanation is that it is no more true than that Larkin was a cretin. I am not alone in remembering that, at the time, he described his visits to Germany with enthusiasm. And if these visits had already 'sowed the seeds' he would not have joined a school party to Belgium for two weeks in 1938; nor, on his return, would he have written for the school magazine an article recounting the fun. He might have been required to accompany his father to Germany; the Belgian trip and his written account of it were voluntary acts.

(One must understand that then, and for some years to come, Larkin had a crippling stammer. I have never known a worse. He himself tells how he would order a ticket at a railway station by writing down his destination. Sustained by his family in Germany or by his schoolmates in Belgium, Larkin could be perfectly happy. Half a mile from his home and alone, he could be distraught. That a stranger might want to reply in a foreign language was of no significance if Larkin could not frame a question anyway. What is impossible cannot be made more difficult.)

By the time Larkin came to leave school he had, saving a couple of boys with a Belgian father and a few Jewish refugees who had begun to turn up, more foreign travel under his belt than any of his school contemporaries; and all the evidence was that he had enjoyed it. Larkin has represented himself as having an indifferent school performance. That was not really true. His grasp of mathematics, and hence of related sciences, was very flimsy. But he was good at languages. Of course he could not master the pronunciation of French, but he could translate into and from it with ease. At Latin he yielded place only to a boy who would go up to Oxford as a classical scholar. Almost his sole recreation was jazz. But not all jazz. When, much later, his stint as jazz critic of a daily newspaper seemed less than successful, it was because he could find little to praise in current jazz offerings. For Larkin, jazz meant Dixieland, Chicago and New York of the 1920s. He knew more about social deprivation in the Deep South than on Clydeside or the Welsh valleys – and I suggest he cared more, too.

The Larkin who went up to Oxford in 1940 was one without any particular animosity to 'abroad' and devoted to an art form that was wholly foreign. It was a wartime Oxford. Personal travel overseas was impossible and, being declared unfit early on for any military service, Larkin neither enjoyed nor endured foreign journeys at the expense of His Majesty. Speculation on life's 'if onlys' is rarely profitable; but because Larkin himself left so few clues, some of which were, anyway, designedly misleading, perhaps this is an area where it might be tried. What if there had been no war in 1939? Larkin was then, as indeed throughout his adult life, deeply respectful of conventions. It was a trait that has commonly been overlooked. (People have often seemed so dazzled by his invariably gaudy socks that they have failed to notice the solid well-made shoes beneath them and the suit of good cloth and traditional cut above.) Now it had been an established Oxford tradition to pass the long vacation in reading parties, frequently, though not invariably, abroad. I have not the least doubt that Larkin would have done the done thing and joined such parties. They would have been the ideal solution to his peculiar problem.

They would have allowed him to do his vacational reading freed from the limitations of his home town and the restrictions of an exceptionally authoritarian parental home. Supported by his friends, he could have lived with his stammer anywhere on the European continent.

By the time the war had ended, Larkin had already embarked on that regular, salaried and pensionable professional employment which so well suited his temperament and in which his father had been such a successful and vigorous exemplar. Foreign travel became possible again. But his father's beloved Germany was in ruins. Foreign currency was severely rationed. Only the most avid travellers ventured abroad.

But in 1950 Larkin took what might, in retrospect, seem a most extraordinary step. He went abroad and lived there. He took a job at the library of Queen's University, Belfast, in the later years of Orange hegemony. He made friends there, of course, as he did everywhere; but it was nevertheless a most disconcerting experience. I recall his telling me with a giggle: 'I never expected to find myself on the side of the Catholics.' I must not be misunderstood. Larkin never doubted that an ordered, hierarchical society, subject to firm government, was in the general interest. In Ulster it seemed not to be working out. Of course, whatever sympathy he might feel for the Catholics in their predicament, he could not approve of their isolating themselves, still less their withholding of political assent. (The IRA had not, at that time, re-emerged; when it did he would abhor it.) All in all, Ulster was a good place not to be and it was with some considerable relief that, in pursuit of his career, he could return to his native country. There were more than enough Catholics in England for Larkin's taste, but at least there was not a government that made you feel you ought to sympathise with them.

That he fetched up in Hull, in 1955, must be attributed, primarily, to the vagaries of job opportunities. But Hull suited him well. The scale of a provincial town with easy access to the sea and to rural Yorkshire was most appealing. In no sense was he a country lad; the excessive intimacy of village life he would have found oppressive; he had no taste for the metropolis. It was in Hull that he consolidated the reputation he had begun to make. In an astonishingly high proportion of his verse the overhang of death is present. The meaning of death was his abiding preoccupation: only find it and the purpose of life would be plain. But if that is your concern, then foreign travel is not going to illuminate it. Take your problem in a rucksack to the Black Forest, or in a suitcase to New York, and it will be exactly the same when you get there; just as, back home again, you will find it unchanged. What won't come from observation and reflection, won't come.

Meantime, the world around Larkin was changing. Europe had made a spectacular recovery. A tourist industry burgeoned. The British flocked abroad for their holidays. This seemed to Larkin, never one to join a herd, a compelling case for staying put. If that made him seem an oddity, he was an even greater one on a university campus. His colleagues were constantly rushing off to symposia and conferences. Prestige attached to a man who could write a paper which, with slight changes here or there, would provide the key to half a dozen academic gatherings in the fleshpots of the world. Larkin would have none of it. It was not that he was without invitations. He turned them all down – but not simply because they might involve foreign travel. He declined invitations to conferences on the same ground that he declined an offer from Auden to support a candidature for the elective Chair of Poetry at Oxford: he wanted to write poetry, not lecture about it.

Precisely because he had become such an oddity, explanations were demanded. What was it that Larkin had against 'abroad'? It was just the sort of question that Larkin would avoid answering. Once you have started explaining yourself, your privacy is endangered, your identity exposed. Much better feed the inquisitive with a diet of extravagances and diversions and if, at the end they remained baffled, well, so much the better. A canard once started can develop its own momentum. And friends might be drafted in to help, perhaps inadvertently. In his review of *Larkin at Sixty* in a daily newspaper, the novelist Anthony Powell wrote that Larkin had 'only once left Great Britain to receive the Shakespeare Prize at Hamburg'. I am sure that Powell wrote what he believed to be true. Because he wrote as a friend (a photograph of Powell standing alongside Larkin was reproduced in the book) Powell's readers would believe it to be true. But we know it wasn't. The error publicly made, was never publicly corrected.

The truth is that Larkin's antipathy to 'abroad' was a fiction. When it suited his pleasure and convenience, he went abroad; when it didn't he stayed at home. What could have been more sensible? But it was never Larkin's purpose to reveal himself. If, as a result, the public were bemused, well, there was sport to be had in keeping them so. Larkin liked a bit of fun.

8

Philip Larkin and Barbara Pym: Two Quiet People

Hazel Holt

On 23 April 1975, in the bar of the Randolph Hotel, Oxford, a novelist and a poet met for the first time.

> I'm sure I should recognise you, but would you know *me*? I am tallish (5.8½ in the old measurements) with darkish brown hair cut short. I shall probably be wearing a beige tweed suit or a Welsh tweed cape if colder. I shall be looking rather anxious, I expect.

> I'm sure we shall recognise each other by progressive elimination, i.e. eliminating all the progressives. I am tall and bald and heavily spectacled and deaf, but I can't predict what I shall have on.[1]

Barbara Pym and Philip Larkin had been corresponding for fourteen years, but this was their first meeting. The Spirit of Irony, never far from Barbara on such occasions, arranged that these two shy, reserved people should be joined by a complete stranger, a jovial red-faced man, the kind who attaches himself to people in hotel bars, who chatted to them for what seemed like hours.

Philip Larkin first wrote to Barbara Pym in 1961, asking when her next novel was to be published and suggesting that he might use the occasion to write a review article about her books in general. Sadly, the 'next novel' was *An Unsuitable Attachment*, which her publishers, Jonathan Cape, rejected and so the article had to wait until 1977 and Barbara's 'rediscovery' before it was written.

Philip had been introduced to Barbara's novels by his sister and was immediately drawn to them. Like him, she too had an 'eye for the small poignancies and comedies of everyday life', and he found them 'heartening and entertaining'.[2] He was, therefore, appalled to hear about her rejection: 'Although she strove to maintain the innocent irony that characterised all her letters, for once it broke down: "I write this calmly enough, but really I was and am very upset about it and think they have treated me very badly."'[3] He was deeply indignant on her behalf: 'It seems a sad state of affairs if such tender, perceptive and intelligent work can't see the light, just because . . . some tasteless chump thinks it won't "go" in paperback.'[4]

Through the following sixteen years, when Barbara could not find a publisher for her books, Philip encouraged and sustained her, partly by writing to her about the work she had in hand, taking her seriously, as one writer to another and, very practically, putting her in touch, with personal recommendations, with those publishers that he knew.

If I or my name can be of any service to you in an introduction of *An Unsuitable Attachment* please let me know.

What do your agreements say? Do the rights revert to you if Cape let the books go out of print? I'm really concerned about it all.

I want these purblind money-mad publishers (Messrs Ginn and Tonnick, Messrs Costa & Brava) to realise how rare and valuable your books are.

I have been re-reading your novels in one fell swoop, whatever that is. . . . Once again I have marvelled at the richness of detail and variety of mood and setting. *Excellent Women* seemed better than I remembered it, full of a kind of harsh suffering very far from the others; it's a study of the pain of being single, the unconscious hurt the world regards as this state's natural clothing – oh dear, this sounds rather extravagant, but time and again one senses not only that Mildred is suffering but that nobody can see why she shouldn't suffer, like a Victorian cabhorse. Don't think I've been concentrating on the dark side: *Some Tame Gazelle* is your *Pride and Prejudice*, rich and untroubled and confident and very funny. John Betjeman was here a few weeks ago and we rejoiced over your work.[5]

It was a heart-lifting experience for a rejected author to think of Britain's two major poets lovingly discussing her novels. Barbara would always have gone on writing, published or not, but such enthusiasm and kindness helped her to maintain in her own mind her status as writer, something very important to one whose confidence had been so badly shaken.

In 1977 *The Times Literary Supplement* asked various notable literary figures to say who they considered to be the most underrated writers of the century. Both Lord David Cecil and Philip Larkin named Barbara Pym. Such is the way of the world, that there was immediately a Pym Revival – her old novels were reprinted and the two new novels that had been rejected by half the publishers in London were suddenly in demand. Almost by accident Philip had helped her at last. He wrote:

Super news! I am drinking (or, come to think of it, have drunk) a half-bottle of champagne in honour of your success. . . . Oh I am so pleased: I want a real Pym year. . . . Apart from the champagne. I have rung up a lady to collect some *jumble* tomorrow for some 'church players' – I've never done this before, so it's *also* in honour of you.[6]

And she replied:

Isn't it splendid the way good news, when you're older, sends you to drink of some kind. . . . (When I was much younger unrequited love caused me to buy and eat half-pound slabs of Cadbury's coffee-milk chocolate.) . . . Of course what I really wanted to know was, what *kind* of jumble, I dare say you'd have some old books from that Library of yours. . . . I haven't *dared* to write to anyone until I actually saw it in print. . . . But now I have the letter [from Macmillan, offering to print *Quartet in Autumn*] before me . . . this is just to say my inadequate thanks. If it hadn't been for you . . . not to mention all those *years* of encouragement. What can I say that would be at all appropriate? I hope anyway that you will be having a *good lunchtime drink*.[7]

As Chairman of the 1977 Booker Committee he was delighted that her new novel *Quartet in Autumn* was short-listed: 'This pretence of making a book on the Booker Award seems either

silly or criminal to me – I could "clean up" . . . if I chose, knowing
the winner. Still, it probably is all a hoax – try your local betting
shop for each way on yourself!'[8]

When Jonathan Cape reprinted her earlier novels Barbara sent
him copies and he replied:

> I am just awaiting the last 15 mins of an Allinson breadmix loaf
> to finish in the oven. . . . and I have heaps to do otherwise, but
> I must thank you *most* warmly for the three lovely books, and
> for troubling to write something different in each one. It really
> is a deep joy for me to contemplate them – not *unmixed* joy,
> because I want to set my teeth in the necks of various publishers
> and shake them like rats – but a great pleasure nonetheless. I
> take a selfish pleasure in seeing my name on them. . . . it's so
> nice to think that good writing wins through in the end. I hope
> your books all sell like billy-o (Brewer is silent on the origin of
> this phrase) and that you have to register for VAT and all that.[9]

Just before she died, Barbara sent Philip copies of the remaining
reissues with her final thanks:

> The whole six really look quite handsome in their bright jackets
> and looking at them perhaps I can quote St Hilda's motto *Non
> frustra vixi* – though I still wonder if any of this would have
> happened if it hadn't been for you and Lord D. And the dear
> *TLS*![10]

Although neither of them had any wish to be part of The
Literary World, both were absorbed by Literature, and Barbara
was naturally interested in Philip as a novelist as well as a poet.

> I was amazed at *Jill*. Such maturity – and detachment and
> 'Sentiments to which every bosom returns an echo . . .' it was
> difficult to believe it had been written by a boy of 21! Of course
> it is very well written and observed too – I don't mean to sound
> surprised at that but I hadn't expected it to be *quite* so good,
> and remembering *A Girl in Winter* one wonders why you didn't
> go on writing fiction, and one regrets it. I suppose you were *too*
> good and didn't perhaps sell enough, and then you preferred
> writing poetry? But couldn't you give us a novel now and

again – those nine years in a northern university . . . surely you are being rather *selfish?*[11]

He admitted that his early ambition had been to write novels, 'but I never got very far'.

I can't bear to look at *A Girl in Winter*: it seems so knowing and smart. I did it when I was about 23, and hoped that I was going to lead that wonderful 500-words-a-day-on-the-Riviera life that beckons us all like an *ignis fatuus* from the age of 16 onwards, but alas I wasn't good enough.[12]

After a while he felt enough at ease with her to write about his poetry:

As usually happens when I am far from my ms book, I feel I could do one or two poems. Let's hope the feeling survives.

I have just written a poem which cheers me slightly, except when I read it, when it depresses me. It's about the sea-side, and rather a self-parody.

Poetry has deserted me – I had a sonnet in the Sheffield *Morning Telegraph* last Saturday, which is how some people *start*, I suppose. Perhaps we shall kick the lids off our tombs simultaneously.

Many thanks for your kind words about the book [*High Windows*]. I wish it were a little bigger and a lot better: one day I hope I can write *happier* poems, but most of the things I think about aren't very cheerful. Perhaps I shall produce a version of *About the House* (Auden's sequence about his Austrian 'pad') [he had just bought 'an ugly little house, frightfully dear'].

Already I find it incredible to be over 50 and 'nothing done', as I feel. In March I shall have been here [Hull] 20 years. . . . In fact I feel somewhat in the doldrums these days: of course *work* goes on, but I am quite unable to do anything in the evenings – the notion of expressing sentiments in short lines having similar sounds at their ends seems as remote as mangoes on the moon.[13]

Of course they both inhabited what Barbara called 'the dustier fringes of the academic world', peopled by librarians, bibliographers and indexers, a constant source of fascinated interest and comedy. She wrote:

> There seems to be more staff in the library [of the International African Institute] than anywhere else – I suppose their purpose is to discourage Visitors. Still I expect that the staff at the University Library Hull do just the same. . . . You will need to gather all your strength for the beginning of your Library extension. . . . I suppose it is a *good* thing that you have joined SCOLMA, which always sounds like a kind of breakfast food or perhaps a tonic for tired academics.[14]

He wrote:

> Our relations [at Hull] with SCOLMA wax and wane. I managed to shift *Liberia* onto the University of London (who had some already) but was then threatened with Madagascar and other small deer.

> My new Library extension is rising slowly . . . . Since about 1961 it's been the daysman of my thought, and hope, and doing.

> My library wasn't quite finished by 1 March, as planned. . . . It's an odd building, of a curious glaring drabness, with far too little staff space, but however. No doubt the students will make it a pretext for some 'polarisation' (the latest word for it) or other when the time comes. I believe 'sit-ins' will replace Rag Week: same time, same general motives. Thank God you aren't in a university! It's like a comprehensive where the kids have never left. . . . I feel deeply humiliated at living in a country that spends more on education than defence.[15]

In her diary Barbara records: 'Philip Larkin sent me a photograph of his new Library extension. Was ever a stranger photo sent by a

man to a woman (in a novel she might be disappointed).'[16]
He had a sharp eye for a 'Barbara Pym situation':

The Warden in a Hall here makes the conference secretary's life a misery with 'several tea pots and hot water jugs were left standing on a polished table last night, instead of being replaced on the tray provided. The table was marked in consequence.'

I feel a fraud as 'Dr' [he had been given an Honorary Doctorate by Queen's University, Belfast, in 1969]. . . . I've *ordered the robes* – only £35 or so. I thought they'd be about £100. I look like Santa Claus in them.

Did I tell you I got my gold medal [for Poetry] through the post? It turned up when I was shaving one morning. Alas for my dreams of entering high society! 'We are told that you are the best poet in our Empire, Mr Larkin' – fat chance.[17]

Needless to say, the last thing either of them ever wanted was any sort of life 'in Society'. When Faber & Faber proposed to put out a new volume of his poems and to reprint *Jill*, Philip wrote:

One day in Spring 1964 the weeklies will have articles headed 'From Immaturity to Decadence', 'A Talent in Decline', 'Gentility's Victim' &c. &c. It is good of you to encourage me in this, but I rather dread it. I have a great shrinking from publicity – think of me as A. E. Housman without the talent or the scholarship, or the soft job, or the curious private life.

I was asked [to the unveiling of the Byron memorial in Westminster Abbey] but since so much of my reputation seems to depend on never being seen anywhere (as meretricious, really, as the reverse, only much pleasanter) I didn't go.

Mrs Gross of *The Observer* came today and 'interviewed' me. I found it very trying – questions about why hadn't I got married, what were my politics, did I think love caused unhappiness, etc. I writhed like a worm on a hook. God knows if it will ever turn into anything. . . . Oh, dear, probably nobody reads these things, but being bibliographed does bring it home that the word sent forth can never be recalled, or whatever the Latin is.

I was somewhat mollified by learning I should be paid! No-one's ever paid me for an interview before, though they take up a hell of a time and are gruelling experiences.[18]

Over the nineteen years of their correspondence a friendship gradually evolved, beginning, as was only to be expected with two such reserved people, very slowly and formally. Thus, nearly three years after his first letter, Barbara wrote: 'May I say "Philip"?, if that is what people call you, or should we go through the academic convention of "Philip Larkin" and "Barbara Pym"?' To which he replied: 'You are welcome to use my Christian name (or forename, as librarians say austerely) – you see, I have ventured to use yours.'[19]

But as time passed, a warmth, and what anthropologists call 'a joking relationship', developed. They shared domestic details with a cheerful cosiness; on her part about jumble sales, church affairs and jokes about constant jam-making: 'The lure of the Seville orange is not to be resisted, and you can cut them up while watching the telly.'[20] On his, the minutiæ of life at Pearson Park:

I have celebrated it [the New Year] by ordering a new gas cooker and a new bedroom carpet. You may wonder what kind of life I lead to wear the existing ones out. In fact my gas cooker was a very small table model and my bedroom has been carpeted for nine years with odd scraps with newspaper underlay. The cooker, the new one, hasn't come yet (it is to be white, not cream, which upset the Gas Board a bit) nor has the carpet, which is a decided yet restful pattern of green leaves. Already the zestful glow that prompted their purchase is fading.[21]

After their first meeting Philip visited Barbara and her sister Hilary at their cottage in Finstock quite often when he was in Oxford. Barbara noted in her diary:

Philip Larkin came to lunch. . . . We ate kipper paté, then veal done with peppers and tomatoes, pommes Anna and celery and cheese (he didn't eat any Brie and we thought perhaps he only likes plain food). He's shy but very responsive and jokey.[22]

But it was not all jumble sales and gas cookers. The feeling and perception which they put into their writing was also part of their lives. From her:

> After all, I have lived eight years since my breast cancer operation in 1971, so I suppose you could say I *have* survived. . . . Of course, 'they' won't tell you how long you've got – it may be several years yet and as I don't want to live to be very old (what one says in middle age anyway!) it is really not so bad. . . . But in some ways you feel a bit foolish, looking and seeming quite well. (What, you *still* here?)[23]

And from him:

> It's been a depressing day. For one thing, my hearing aid has gone wrong again. . . . I'm beginning to feel, as it cost £80, a bit of a mug. (I forget if I've ever said that one of the few blessings of my advancing age is a merciful blurring of the sounds around me.) Then, one *does* get depressed sometimes, has anyone ever done any work on why memories are always unhappy? I don't mean really unhappy, as of blacking factories, but sudden stabbing memories of especially absurd and painful moments that one is suffused and excoriated by – I have a dozen, some 30 years old, some a year or even less, and once one arrives, all the rest follow. I suppose if one lives to be old one's entire waking life will be spent turning on the spit of recollection over the fires of mingled shame, pain and remorse. Cheerful prospect! Why can't I recall the pleasure of hearing my Oxford results, having my novel accepted, passing my driving test – things such as these? Life doesn't work like that.[24]

After the posthumous publication of Barbara's diaries in *A Very Private Eye* Philip wrote to me:

> My impression. . . . is of the sadness of it all – the literary rejection, the ill health and ageing. Yet she is simultaneously so tough and perceptive with it that one's attention is easily distracted by the 'Elderly ladies, coughing and cackling' and the overheard conversations, coming back only when another blow falls.[25]

But they shared many happy moments, and perhaps the one we would choose to remember is recorded in Barbara's diary entry for 30 July 1976:

> Philip Larkin came to tea then walked up to the church to see the T. S. Eliot memorial. So two great poets and one minor novelist came for a brief moment (as it were) together. Philip took photos of us all with two cats outside the cottage. What is the point of saying (as if for posterity) what Philip is *like*. He is so utterly what he is in his letters and poems. In the best like 'Faith healing', 'Ambulances', and even Jake Balokowsky, my biographer. 'Life at graduate level' as he once said about my novel *No Fond Return*.

Part Two
His Work

9

Larkin's Presence

William H. Pritchard

'I think in one sense I'm like Evelyn Waugh or John Betjeman, in that there's not much to say about my work. When you've read a poem, that's it, it's all quite clear what it means.'[1] Thus Philip Larkin, parrying an interviewer's asking whether he had profited from reading criticism of himself. One takes the point: this is a poet who made every effort, and successfully, not to write poems that – as he said Emily Dickinson's too often did – 'expire in a teased-out and breathless obscurity'.[2] And even though relative obscurity can occasionally be found in Larkin's poetry, especially in earlier work like 'Dry-Point' and 'Latest Face' from *The Less Deceived*, his poems typically have 'plots', are narratives with beginning, middle and end, spoken by a voice that invites trust (though not all speakers in his poems are trustworthy) and seeks what Frost said good poems issued in – a 'clarification of life'. Not necessarily, as Frost went on to say, 'a great clarification, such as sects and cults are founded on', but 'a momentary stay against confusion'.[3]

Larkin's remark about his poems being so clear in what they mean that there's not much to say about them should not however be dismissed – like Waugh's responses to interviewers – as merely a way of eluding questions. Not that he's above discomfiting the questioner, as when, asked what he had learned from his 'study' of Auden, Yeats and Hardy, he snapped back with 'Oh, for Christ's sake, one doesn't *study* poets! You *read* them, and think, That's marvellous, how is it done, could I do it?' (The best riposte to one of his parryings was Auden's. After asking Larkin how he liked living in Hull and having Larkin reply that he was no unhappier there than any other place, Auden clucked at him 'Naughty, Naughty'.[4]) But a glance at criticism of the poems doesn't reveal interpretive disputes about them or strikingly divergent notions of which are the best ones. It seems generally agreed that his poetic output, if small, was distinguished; that

71

whether his range is thought to be relatively narrow or wide as life itself, the poems are like nobody else's. If there are readers of poetry in England and America who don't at all share these sentiments, they have kept quiet about their dissent. But if indeed there's 'not much to say' about the poems – as there is, for example, a great deal to say about James Merrill's poems: charting allusions, sizing up the tone of a line, proposing and correcting particular 'readings' – there may yet be something of interest to be said about the challenge Larkin's work presents to contemporary ideas about poets and poetry. This would require an attempt to characterise the reader of Larkin who feels that this challenge is a splendid thing to have occurred. And with Larkin more than with most poets the challenge is one the reader takes personally: why does this body of work matter so much to *me*?

More than thirty years ago Randall Jarrell said in a letter to James Agee that writing poetry involved one in struggling 'both against the current of the world and the current of the World of Poetry, a small world much more interested in Wallace Stevens than in Chekhov, Homer, and Wordsworth combined'.[5] Looking around him, shortly before the publication of Ginsberg's *Howl* and the domestic poems of Lowell's *Life Studies*, Jarrell saw in American poets under forty (he had just turned that corner) what he called 'the world of Richard Wilbur and safer paler mirror-images of Richard Wilbur' – the era of 'the poet in the grey-flannel suit'. Three years later, looking through an anthology of English and American poets under forty, he saw little to contradict his picture of poets and poems that didn't take enough chances: *New Poets of England and America* (ed. Hall, Pack, and Simpson) mainly presented – and seems three decades later still to present – work for which the word accomplished comes all too readily to mind. Yet in that anthology Jarrell found and read with pleasure seven poems by Philip Larkin, including 'Church Going', 'Poetry of Departures', and 'At Grass', from *The Less Deceived*. (The book had not yet been published in America, but serious readers of poetry knew about it in the late 1950s, when it could be ordered from England for ten shillings and sixpence.) Lowell, then well into his *Life Studies* poems in the new style – he included a version of 'Skunk Hour' in a letter to Jarrell about the anthology – told him that he had been reading Larkin since the previous spring and liked him better than anyone since Dylan Thomas, indeed liked him better than Thomas. He was not only the most interesting of the 'movement' poets, but 'unlike our smooth younger poets says something'. In reply, Jarrell said he was 'delighted' with the remark about Larkin, since he himself was 'crazy about him'.

I mention this little episode in literary history to point out that for all the critical tendency to patronise Larkin as a wistful ineffectual angel ('He is plain and passive . . . a sympathetic figure as he stands at the window, trying not to cloud it with his breath'[6]), his voice in its early manifestations struck two of the best American poets as a fresh accent, put to the service of saying something, as in the opening of 'Poetry of Departures':

> Sometimes you hear, fifth-hand,
> As epitaph:
> *He chucked up everything*
> *And just cleared off,*
> And always the voice will sound
> Certain you approve
> This audacious, purifying,
> Elemental move.

The voice's accent commands not only a lively, slangy idiom in which chuckings up and clearings off are at home, but in addition a cool Latinate superiority to people who get so excited about that idiom that they can't imagine anyone hearing it in a different way. Having so deftly laid down those ironic adjectives – 'audacious', 'purifying', 'elemental' – so as seemingly to kill any pretensions to value the 'move' might have, Larkin then changes perspective, appearing to entertain a second thought and what follows from it. For the rest of the poem it's impossible to consider stanzas separately since the voice moves through and over them with quietly dazzling changes of pace:

> And they are right, I think.
> We all hate home
> And having to be there:
> I detest my room,
> Its specially-chosen junk,
> The good books, the good bed,
> And my life, in perfect order:
> So to hear it said

> *He walked out on the whole crowd*
> Leaves me flushed and stirred,
> Like *Then she undid her dress*
> Or *Take that you bastard*;
> Surely I can, if he did?
> And that helps me stay
> Sober and industrious.
> But I'd go today,
>
> Yes, swagger the nut-strewn roads,
> Crouch in the fo'c'sle
> Stubbly with goodness, if
> It weren't so artificial,
> Such a deliberate step backwards
> To create an object:
> Books; china; a life
> Reprehensibly perfect.

In reading the poem aloud or typing it out, one discovers just how perfect an object it is, though not 'reprehensibly' so. Although I don't propose to talk about Larkin's rhyming, it should at least be acknowledged as the operation that makes everything come together and cohere (as it does with his early master Yeats and his later master Hardy). In 'Poetry of Departures' there are full rhymes usually at the end of a stanza (approve/move; bed/said; stay/today), Audenesque off-rhymes (there/order; think/junk; if/life), and comic-looking or sounding ones that vary depending on your Anglo or American pronunciation (epitaph/off; stirred/bastard – in his recording of the poem Larkin pronounced it bah-stud, which makes for a wholly engaging ring).

For all its talk of undone dresses and bastards, 'Poetry of Departures' recalls no modern poet more than Frost, not just because Larkin refuses to trade in 'the deliberate step backwards' for the call of the wild (Frost wrote a poem titled 'One Step Backward Taken'), but for the way both poets need to plant themselves firmly someplace so that they can compellingly imagine someplace else. Frost's charming poem about Henry Hudson ('I stay;/But it isn't as if/There wasn't always Hudson's Bay') is titled 'An Empty Threat' but the threat of departure, however empty, is enough to fill a poem with detail after imagined detail. The same for Larkin, whose little poem of departure plays with the notion of walking out on things, something he can imagine doing only when he has his feet still in the middle of them. Frost is one of the poets from this century, along with Hardy, Sassoon, Edward Thomas, Betjeman and Wilfred Owen, whom Larkin said he kept within reach of his working chair (no Auden? no Graves?), but it is important that their affinity not be seen to consist in the way they both expunge romantic possibilities from their consciousness. They may – or at least Larkin did – have expunged them from their lives, but only the better to entertain them in their writing.

John Bayley, who has written about Larkin with his usual perceptiveness, calls this temperamental inclination by the title of a poem from *The Whitsun Weddings*, 'The Importance of Elsewhere', and calls Larkin also, with Keats and Yeats in the background, the last Romantic. As with Keats – and probably Yeats too, as it was for D. H. Lawrence who made up the phrase – Larkin's was a case of 'sex in the head', or so he would have us believe from the things he said in print. For him, says Bayley, 'The erotic is elsewhere and evaporates on consummation'. And with Keats's 'Lamia' and Larkin's first novel *Jill* in mind, Bayley suggests that 'the man who creates and contemplates romance is extinguished by its realization or fulfilment'.[7] Larkin uses that last word at the end of 'No Road', one of a number of poems in *The Less Deceived* that speak, with an unmistakably personal ring, about a relationship between two people which didn't pan out and after which, the poet imagines, time will obliterate the already disused road between them:

> To watch that world come up like a cold sun,
> Rewarding others, is my liberty.
> Not to prevent it is my will's fulfilment.
> Willing it, my ailment.

The poems he wrote were good for what ailed him. Another way of making the same point about life was to reply, as Larkin did when asked if he were happy, that yes he was but that one couldn't write poems about being happy: 'Deprivation is for me what daffodils were for Wordsworth',[8] was his happy formulation. In other words, you can and cannot know me through my poems.

Along with sex, the richest 'elsewhere' in Larkin's experience

was American jazz, even as he listened to plenty of it. For him
and Kingsley Amis as Oxford undergraduates,

> Russell, Charles Ellsworth 'Pee Wee' (b. 1906), clarinet and
> saxophone player extraordinary, was, *mutatis mutandis*, our
> Swinburne and our Byron. We bought every record he played
> on that we could find, and – literally – dreamed about similar
> items on the American Commodore label.[9]

This was no charming exaggeration; Larkin and Amis may have
had better ears than any other recent English writers (or is it just
that my own ear is tuned to them?), and I can't believe it had
nothing to do with how much jazz, Pee Wee Russell and the rest,
they listened to. The whole of English poetry was available there
in the Bodleian, yet think of all those American Commodore jazz
records that were elsewhere, the ones they hadn't heard. Although
at Oxford, as in other places, jazz was and is a minority taste, its
being more exciting than poetry surely had to do with this relative
inaccessibility. Anyone who once yearned to possess sides or
albums the record companies had let go out of print (things are
better these days) knows what the excitement of such an elsewhere
can feel like.

But it wasn't only the music that interested Larkin. Even before
he discovered jazz he had listened to dance music, dance bands,
and said that he must have learned 'dozens of dance lyrics' about
which he said to an interviewer that

> I suppose they were a kind of folk poetry. Some of them were
> pretty awful, but I often wonder whether my assumption that a
> poem is something that rhymes and scans didn't come from
> listening to them – and some of them were quite sophisticated.
> 'The Venus de Milo was noted for her charms/But strictly
> between us, you're cuter than Venus/And what's more you've
> got arms' – I can't imagine Mick Jagger singing that; you know,
> it was witty and technically clever.[10]

The lines about the Venus de Milo, from 'Love Is Just Around the
Corner', seem to have been favourites since he mentions them
more than once, and the influence of dance lyrics may be
observed, not merely in the fact that Larkin's poems rhyme and
scan, but in how they sound, the way – line by line – they swing.

There is no better place to observe such a movement than in the opening poem from *The Less Deceived*, the one that thirty years ago introduced this reader to Larkin. 'Lines on a Young Lady's Photograph Album' says more about looking at photographs than any poem I know, and it also investigates what it means to pore over the snapped stages of someone whose past you care about:

> My swivel eye hungers from pose to pose –
> In pigtails, clutching a reluctant cat;
> Or furred yourself, a sweet girl-graduate;
> Or lifting a heavy-headed rose
> Beneath a trellis, or in a trilby hat
>
> (Faintly disturbing, that, in several ways) –
> From every side you strike at my control,
> Not least through these disquieting chaps who loll
> At ease about your earlier days:
> Not quite your class, I'd say, dear, on the whole.

The movement of these stanzas is of course more complicated and 'unsingable' than dance tunes can afford to be – consider the pauses within the lines, the way cat/graduate slightly off-rhymes, the parenthetical irony. Yet there are also memorable solo lines that seem to have come out of some Golden Treasury of Popular Song: 'From every side you strike at my control' or 'Not quite your class, I'd say, dear, on the whole' – surely Fred Astaire sang them in some 1930s movie? And there is a distinctly Cole Porterish feeling in a later stanza, which, after insisting that the photographs have persuaded him 'That this is a real girl in a real place', goes on to speculate about whether and how much the truth of those images is dependent on their original being no longer present:

> In every sense empirically true!
> Or is it just *the past*? Those flowers, that gate,
> These misty parks and motors, lacerate
> Simply by being over; you
> Contract my heart by looking out of date.

Witty and technically accomplished certainly, but also poignant the way a gorgeous line can be, this last one delivered, again, with the wistful elegance of an Astaire, maybe a Billie Holiday.

(And note the wonderful bonus provided by the double sense of 'contract'.) When Louis MacNeice died in 1963, Larkin wrote a short appreciation for the *New Statesman* in which he called MacNeice a 'town observer' whose poetry was the poetry of everyday life. But beyond that poetry's treatment of shop-windows and lawnmowers and its 'uneasy awareness of what the newsboys were shouting', MacNeice, he wrote, 'displayed a sophisticated sentimentality about falling leaves and lipsticked cigarette stubs: he could have written the words of "These Foolish Things"'.[11] A lovely tribute which might well be paid to Larkin himself, especially in his earlier poems.

All the best ones from *The Less Deceived*, including of course the best known of all, 'Church Going', are poems of tenderness directed at something that is now elsewhere. Their need is nothing so clearly identifiable as nostalgia; nobody who took Larkin's sardonic, unillusioned view of his own childhood can be accused of that:

> By now I've got the whole place clearly charted.
> Our garden, first: where I did not invent
> Blinding theologies of flowers and fruits,
> And wasn't spoken to by an old hat.
>   ('I Remember, I Remember')

He doesn't write poems out of the feeling that – as in a line from Jarrell – 'In those days everything was better'. It is rather the difference between now and then (most affectingly expressed in 'MCMXIV' from *The Whitsun Weddings*) that moves him and animates a poem. In speaking about something that is elsewhere – maybe past and gone but not quite – Larkin achieves an extraordinary intimacy of tone, both in relation to that subject and to the implicated reader, who, it is assumed, will care just as much about it as the poet does. (His rhetoric never insists on how really splendid something is, in fact.) Think of this passage about a married woman's maiden name:

> Now it's a phrase applicable to no one,
> Lying just where you left it, scattered through
> Old lists, old programmes, a school prize or two,
> Packets of letters tied with tartan ribbon –
> Then is it scentless, weightless, strengthless, wholly

Untruthful? Try whispering it slowly.
No, it means you. Or, since you're past and gone,

It means what we feel now about you then:
How beautiful you were, and near, and young.
('Maiden Name')

Jarrell once wrote that 'the poem is a love affair between the poet
and his subject, and readers come in only a long time later, as
witnesses at the wedding'.[12] Such a poetry has its sudden
intimacies of tone ('No, it means you'), and – in case there are
people who think Larkin's voice lacked passion – its certifiable
intensities of feeling, of love, are witnessed by us.

Unlike the almost forgotten maiden name Larkin writes a poem
to revive, a name can live on while the bearer of it is forgotten,
and Larkin can right that balance too, as in the final poem from
The Less Deceived about once-famous racehorses now subsided into
something else. 'The eye can hardly pick them out', 'At Grass'
begins, but by the fourth stanza Larkin has achieved a beautiful
feeling for his subject, those horses who are wholly unaware of
his questioning of them:

> Do memories plague their ears like flies?
> They shake their heads. Dusk brims the shadows.
> Summer by summer all stole away,
> The starting-gates, the crowds and cries –
> All but the unmolesting meadows.
> Almanacked, their names live; they
>
> Have slipped their names, and stand at ease.

The touch is so sure that one almost misses the point that those
horses shake their heads not to assure the poet they're impervious
to memory but merely to twitch away the flies that are plaguing
them. About the surprising 'unmolesting', as modifying the
meadows, faithful in their way to the otherwise deserted horses,
one can only say with Larkin, who, when asked how he'd arrived
at an image in his poem 'Toads', answered, 'Sheer genius'.

These poems and others from *The Less Deceived* speak to the
reader's own need to be less deceived – the need to be intimate
with the past and with loss (of a maiden name, of how one used

to look, of a horse's once thoroughbred performance) by seizing them through the poet's words. There is little to be done about the present except to endure it as it erodes us; Frost's lines from 'Carpe Diem'[13] say what there is to be said on the subject:

> But bid life seize the present?
> It lives less in the present
> Than in the future always,
> And less in both together
> Than in the past. The present
> Is too much for the senses,
> Too crowding, too confusing –
> Too present to imagine.

And when Larkin decides to live for a bit in the future, the consequences are predictably grim, the end of England foreseen:

> For the first time I feel somehow
> That it isn't going to last,
>
> That before I snuff it, the whole
> Boiling will be bricked in
> Except for the tourist parts –
> First slum of Europe: . . .
> > ('Going, Going')

But on occasion he succeeds magnificently in imagining the crowding, confusing present by writing a poetry of becoming, of flux, and by exulting in the process rather than lamenting it. 'Wedding-Wind' (an early, Lawrentian poem) and 'Coming' from *The Less Deceived*, 'Here' and 'Water' from *The Whitsun Weddings*, are examples of such imaginings. And in the second section of 'Livings', from *High Windows*, an unidentified speaker, evidently a lighthouse keeper, raptly contemplates a vividly present scene:

> Seventy feet down
> The sea explodes upwards,
> Relapsing, to slaver
> Off landing-stage steps –
> Running suds, rejoice!

Rocks writhe back to sight.
Mussels, limpets,
Husband their tenacity
In the freezing slither –
Creatures, I cherish you!

It is a remarkably early-Audenesque telegram in which the importance of elsewhere is subordinated to the here-and-now:

Radio rubs its legs,
Telling me of elsewhere:

Barometers falling,
Ports wind-shuttered,
Fleets pent like hounds,
Fires in humped inns
Kippering sea-pictures –

Keep it all off!

Without the author's name attached, no one would guess this was Larkin; its language revels in the attempt to live up to, even outdo, the invigorating chaos of the world it embodies.

A similar, and similarly rich, satisfaction – though most mutedly expressed – occurs when a scene or place in the present engages him because the life has gone out of it, has gone elsewhere. Yet, as with Wordsworth looking at London from Westminster Bridge before anyone is stirring, the place now offers its essential being, seen as if truly for the first time. In 'Friday Night in the Royal Station Hotel',

Light spreads darkly downwards from the high
Cluster of lights over empty chairs
That face each other, coloured differently.
Through open doors, the dining-room declares
A larger loneliness of knives and glass
And silence laid like carpet. A porter reads
An unsold evening paper. Hours pass,
And all the salesmen have gone back to Leeds,
Leaving full ashtrays in the Conference Room.

In shoeless corridors, the lights burn. How
Isolated, like a fort, it is –
The headed paper, made for writing home
(If home existed) letters of exile: *Now*
Night comes on. Waves fold behind villages.

I suppose that down through the line comparing the hotel to a
fort one might call the poem merely expert, the sort of thing one
comes to expect from Larkin-on-emptiness. But where on earth
did the italicised message come from, imagined to be written
home by the imaginary exile? It moves the poem beyond expertise
into the surprising, unsettling creation Larkin at his best is capable
of.

'Livings' (part II) and 'Friday Night in the Royal Station Hotel'
offer us, if you will, glimpses of the Sublime; but sometimes
Larkin invites us into a present, at least for a moment, by
achieving what a student of mine cleverly called The Tacky
Sublime. In 'The Large Cool Store' we are shown how most of the
'cheap clothes' match the workday habits of the working class
people who buy them. Then there is a surprise:

But past the heaps of shirts and trousers
Spread the stands of Modes For Night:
Machine-embroidered, thin as blouses,

Lemon, sapphire, moss-green, rose
Bri-Nylon Baby-Dolls and Shorties
Flounce in clusters . . .

Yet this satiric vision of loveliness leads not to further satiric
treatment, but rather to a serious meditation on how hard it is to
say something conclusive about women and love.

Some of Larkin's best work is to be found in each of the three
books of poetry he published at ten-year intervals (I am excluding
his early *The North Ship* as not the real thing), and the finest of the
three is the last, *High Windows*. Perhaps, with T. S. Eliot in mind
he scoffed at the notion of a poet's 'development' (to Ian Hamilton
in an interview he quoted Oscar Wilde's line about only
mediocrities developing). But *High Windows*, with only twenty-
four poems, is the quintessence of all the books and contains four
of his richest and most ample works: 'To the Sea'; 'The Old Fools';

'The Building'; and 'Show Saturday' (with Yeats-like stanzas of nine, twelve, seven and eight lines respectively). Along with his final poem, 'Aubade', 'The Old Fools' and 'The Building' are the darkest, most death-oriented poems he wrote; the other two are equally life-affirming in their blessings on two rituals – going to the beach, going to the fair. 'Show Saturday', with its elaborately rhymed stanzas that enjamb themselves one into the next, concludes in a burst of – for Larkin – positively positive thinking, saluting with alliterative energy the 'dismantled Show', now concluded but to return next year, same time:

> Let it stay hidden there like strength, below
> Sale-bills and swindling; something people do,
> Not noticing how time's rolling smithy-smoke
> Shadows much greater gestures; something they share
> That breaks ancestrally each year into
> Regenerate union. Let it always be there.

Larkin is not, of course, exactly 'there', nor is he one of the bathers in 'To the Sea' who persist in making another kind of annual show:

> If the worst
> Of flawless weather is our falling short,
> It may be that through habit these do best,
> Coming to water clumsily undressed
> Yearly; teaching their children by a sort
> Of clowning; helping the old, too, as they ought.

These are the sort of people an Auberon Waugh recoils from in disgust; Larkin gives them his considered respect.

As for the dark poems, 'The Building' and 'The Old Fools' lose none of their original terror – it is not too strong a word – on rereading. The first is an improvisation, in the mode of Kafka or Fellini, on this unnamed structure (to call it a hospital would be to commit the Jamesian sin of weak specification) which signals that 'something has gone wrong':

> It must be error of a serious sort,
> For see how many floors it needs, how tall
> It's grown by now, and how much money goes

In trying to correct it. See the time,
Half-past eleven on a working day,
And these picked out of it; see, as they climb

To their appointed levels, how their eyes
Go to each other, guessing; on the way
Someone's wheeled past, in washed-to-rags ward clothes:
They see him, too. They're quiet. To realise
This new thing held in common makes them quiet,
For past these doors are rooms, and rooms past those,
And more rooms yet . . .

The neutral tone belies the hopeless subject: it is as if Larkin has
to keep writing in the hope that, for the space of the poem, he can
help us fend off the hopelessness. By contrast, 'The Old Fools' is
more compact and more tonally aggressive, especially in its first
two stanzas, at the expense of age's incapacity to know what's
happening to it ('Do they somehow suppose / It's more grown-up
when your mouth hangs open and drools, / And you keep on
pissing yourself, and can't remember / Who called this morning?').
But by the third stanza, in a moment of sympathetic identification
the poet makes up for his would-be callousness, giving the old
fools some metaphors with which to see themselves:

Perhaps being old is having lighted rooms
Inside your head, and people in them, acting.
People you know, yet can't quite name; each looms
Like a deep loss restored, from known doors turning,
Setting down a lamp, smiling from a stair, extracting
A known book from the shelves; or sometimes only
The rooms themselves, chairs and a fire burning,
The blown bush at the window, or the sun's
Faint friendliness on the wall some lonely
Rain-ceased midsummer evening. That is where they live:
Not here and now, but where all happened once.
        This is why they give

An air of baffled absence, trying to be there
Yet being here . . .

It is, I think, Larkin's most handsome stanza (comparable to it are the final ones from 'The Whitsun Weddings' and 'Dockery and Son'), and it encloses perhaps the most beautifully realised and affecting sequence in all his work. The poem doesn't quite end there, and the horror of enduring this 'whole hideous inverted childhood' returns, now with the poet including himself in it: 'Well, we shall find out.' It is the last answer, if another were needed, to Browning's salute to age in 'Rabbi Ben Ezra', and not just one further voice in an argument about growing old but a crushing unanswerable statement of fact. Perhaps too crushing, one might argue – too sweeping, too exclusively grim in its portraiture; yet it has a lot of truth going for it. As Lowell remarked, a poem by Larkin 'says something'.[14] 'The Old Fools' says something final about what was always his ultimate subject.

For if Larkin was driven to write about love consummated elsewhere, the young in one another's arms ('Sexual intercourse began/In nineteen sixty-three/(Which was rather late for me) –', then old age and the death about which 'We shall find out' was even more irresistible as a subject to be fetched from elsewhere and entertained in the poem. Larkin 'developed' into the poet who wrote 'The Old Fools' by taking life – as Frost said poetry should – by the throat, exaggerating both his disgust at old-age horrors and his sympathetic tenderness for those people with lighted rooms inside their heads. It issues in a memorableness that has nothing in common with A. Alvarez's calling him the poet of 'suburban hermitage . . . and all mod con'.[15] 'Death kills a man; the idea of death saves him', said Forster in *Howards End* perhaps too chirpily, at least too much so for Larkin, who wasn't about to talk about salvation in any terms. There is testimony in Andrew Motion's fine memorial poem about him, 'This is Your Subject Speaking',[16] that he refused to talk about salvation as being somehow possible through art. In that poem Larkin, visiting Motion for supper, comes across a book-mark which says 'Some say/Life's the thing, but I prefer reading', and snaps back:

> *Jesus Christ what balls.* You spun
> round on your heel to the table
> almost before your anger took hold . . .

Later, cooled down, 'Larkin' goes on to say:

> *You see, there's nothing to write*
> *Which is better than life itself, no matter*
> *how life might let you down, or pass you by . . .*

This speaking up for life might have taken a sharper edge as he saw his own powers as a poet disappearing. In 1982 he ended his *Paris Review* interview with the terse declaration: 'It's unlikely I shall write any more poems' (not many, *any*)[17] and at another moment in Motion's poem he says to the younger man

> *Don't ask me*
> *Why I stopped, I didn't stop. It stopped.*
> *In the old days I'd go home at six*
> *and write all evening on a board*
>
> *across my knees. But now . . . I go home*
> *and there's nothing there. I'm like a chicken*
> *with no egg to lay.*

His last egg, as it were, was one of his very best. 'Aubade', published in December of 1977, was written as death in its elsewhereness seemed closer, staying in the poem's words 'just on the edge of Vision':

> I work all day, and get half drunk at night.
> Waking at four to soundless dark, I stare.
> In time the curtain-edges will grow light.
> Till then I see what's really always there:
> Unresting death, a whole day nearer now.
> Making all thought impossible but how
> And where and when I shall myself die.
> Arid interrogation: yet the dread
> Of dying, and of being dead,
> Flashes afresh to hold and horrify.

Here, unlike 'The Old Fools', the personal edge is felt at the very beginning and only deepens over the poem's five stanzas. It is nothing more than mere total emptiness that horrifies him – 'nothing more terrible, nothing more true' – and in the third stanza, with a touch of the younger, slangier Oxford iconoclast, he sees through the religious consolation:

That vast moth-eaten musical brocade
Created to pretend we never die,
And specious stuff that says *No rational being*
Can fear a thing it will not feel, not seeing
That this is what we fear – no sight, no sound,
No touch or taste or smell, nothing to think with,
Nothing to love or link with,
The anaesthetic from which none come round.

The voice rises, with pressing excitement, to 'correct' the blindness of consolatory wisdom that doesn't know the half of it, of the 'Waking to soundless dark' at four a.m. which he has just undergone and which is his undressed rehearsal for the grave. Since 'Death is no different whined at than withstood', the poem ends in a getting up, a coming back without illusion to life, which like death had better not be either whined at nor withstood, but rather just met:

Slowly light strengthens, and the room takes shape.
It stands plain as a wardrobe, what we know,
Have always known, know that we can't escape,
Yet can't accept. One side will have to go.
Meanwhile telephones crouch, getting ready to ring
In locked-up offices, and all the uncaring
Intricate rented world begins to rouse.
The sky is white as clay, with no sun.
Work has to be done.
Postmen like doctors go from house to house.

Those three single-line concluding sentences, in which the 'intricate, rented world' is faced (and what a stroke that 'rented' is), are the point in his work beyond which Larkin was not to go, and perhaps for strong reasons. If a poet has to stop writing there is justice for it happening in coincidence with his subject: to maul slightly Emily Dickinson's line, Larkin's work could stop for death. 'Most poets have nothing to write about'. James Dickey once confided.[18] Larkin knew what he had to write about and when he had done it.

One's response to his death in December of 1985 was then, for all the sense of loss, not a sense that had he lived he would have gone on to write poems he had not quite yet grown into writing.

(It would be nice to have been wrong and to have seen him live
and write on so as to prove it.) For essentially his work felt
complete – as Jarrell's did after *The Lost World* or Bishop's after
Geography III, or as Lowell's did perhaps even before he published
Day by Day. On the face of it nothing could be more absurd than
to compare the four slim volumes Larkin gave us (counting *The
North Ship* this time) with the eight individually much larger ones
of his ancestral favourite, Hardy; yet if Hardy's emergence as a
poet is dated from *Wessex Poems* (1898), both he and Larkin
(dating from *The North Ship*, 1945) had some thirty years of
production. We know that Larkin put himself on record as not
wishing Hardy's vast collection a single poem shorter, and as
calling his work 'many times over' the best body of poetry in the
century.[19] One of the pleasures in re-reading Hardy is of course
the discovery of poems one had previously missed, or only half-
read: compared, say, to Eliot, he seems inexhaustible. How many
re-readers of Larkin's books have a similar feeling? I think I know
his poems as well as those of any postmodern poet; still, to re-
read is to be struck not by their being fewer than 100 poems all
told in *The Less Deceived*, *The Whitsun Weddings* and *High Windows*,
but by the density and weight of the ones there are.

How much this has to do with their being poems of great
formal craft, especially (and frequently) in their often elaborately-
schemed rhyme and stanzas, is hard to specify. My feeling is that
the craft has a great deal, maybe everything to do with it. When
compared to two very different contemporary poets of reputation,
John Ashberry and Adrienne Rich, the difference Larkin's
adherence to traditional metric, stanzas and rhyme makes is
patent. Ashberry may well possess, as David Bromwich has
declared, the 'original idiom of our times', but as his prolific
output testifies it may not take quite as much care or time to write
a poem if one doesn't require rhyme and stanza, and if one is
more concerned with nonsense than with sense. (I can't believe
that Larkin was not making pointed mischief when he said –
explaining why his bad hearing kept him from travelling to
America – 'Someone would say Ashberry, and I'd say, I'd prefer
strawberry, that sort of thing.'[20]) And it is hard to imagine
Adrienne Rich discovering that her poetry had just dried up, that
(in the phrase from Motion's poem about Larkin) she had become
a chicken with no egg to lay. There will always be some new or
old issue of gender and power on which to exercise her poetic will

in various free forms. Ashberry and Rich have written many books of poetry; we may see Larkin's relatively few against the background of the formal tests he set for himself in drawing the figures of poems.

The craft, the elegance, the ceaseless wit – how could anyone say, as W. J. Bate and David Perkins do in their recent anthology of British and American poets, that Larkin writes 'the poetry of personal statement and dreary realism'?[21] Although thirty years ago Jarrell hailed him as the antidote to 'the world of Richard Wilbur',[22] it is Wilbur, born just a year before Larkin, to whom he can be compared in his command of syntax and suppleness and tone. Larkin might not have liked the comparison, might have felt Wilbur more of a high-toned formalist than he. But for all the American poet's fastidious good manners (those who don't much like him call it primness), Wilbur's poetry from *Ceremony* through *The Mind-Reader* unmistakably reveals a distinct presence, a person whose character and inclinations we get to know very well. If Wilbur, in Brad Leithauser's phrase, is 'one of the few living American masters of formal verse',[23] then Larkin was its most recent English master of such verse. And for all its difference from Wilbur's, his poetry shows a person at least as distinct in his outlines, his tastes, the clarity of his idiom. Either of them could have written the next to last poem in Larkin's last book:

> Cut grass lies frail:
> Brief is the breath
> Mown stalks exhale.
> Long, long the death
>
> It dies in the white hours
> Of young-leafed June
> With chestnut flowers,
> With hedges snowlike strewn,
>
> White lilac bowed,
> Lost lanes of Queen Anne's lace,
> And that high-builded cloud
> Moving at summer's pace.

In the fewest possible words, 'Cut Grass' says much, surely enough to serve as a poet's epitaph.

10

Philip Larkin: Voices and Values

J. R. Watson

Philip Larkin had a good voice. By that I mean that it was effective in conveying his meaning, agreeable to listen to, and capable of registering different shades of feeling with some sensitivity. Although he suffered from a stammer at one period of his life, he controlled his voice so well during his mature years that its hesitations became almost undetectable; and his reading and speaking voice had an instantly pleasing, even winning quality about it. It was also, as some voices are, instantly recognisable: it was Philip's voice, and no one else's, and as we lament his death we may well realise the sensitivity of Tennyson's

> But O for the touch of a vanish'd hand,
> And the sound of a voice that is still!

The listener could reflect upon this during the memorial service for Philip Larkin in Westminster Abbey, where the voices were fine and memorable, but where there was always the bleak absence of *that* voice, the recognisable, identifiable sound of the poet himself. It was made more poignant by Ted Hughes's reading of the magnificent chapter 44 of Ecclesiasticus, a reading that was full of energy and character, with nothing of the Anglican plumminess about it: 'men renowned for their power', he read 'giving counsel by their understanding', and the word 'counsel' came across as 'cownsell', Yorkshire-strong and clean as a dry-stone wall. Then Jill Balcon read three of Philip's poems, 'Love Songs in Age', 'Church Going', and 'An Arundel Tomb': her reading was very beautiful, indeed faultless, but behind it, all the time, the inner ear heard that other voice, familiar from the records, unique and irreplaceable, if only because it was so rich with the accumulated experience that shaped the poems

90

themselves. In Dylan Thomas's work, wrote Philip, 'the voice and the style are indissoluble',[1] and earlier in the same essay he observed that 'a poet always thinks of his poems as being read in his own voice'.[2] Since the coming of the gramophone and the tape recorder, his readers (listeners) do, too.

It is that voice which makes Philip Larkin's poems different from those of his contemporaries, even from those of John Betjeman which he so loved and admired. Bill Ruddick has recently drawn attention to the echoes of Betjeman in Larkin's poetry,[3] but Betjeman's voice was very different; it never lost that self-indulgent nursery and prep-school quality which was then mixed with old-fashioned Oxford-isms – 'orf' and 'crors' instead of 'off' and 'cross'. When Larkin picked up echoes and resonances from Betjeman, he transformed the echo into a different sound. The difference is important, not because of the social or sociological matters which are involved, but because of the sheer individuality and difference of the listening experience: however much we may find Betjeman, or others, in the poetry of Larkin, the words when spoken by the one have a different quality from the same words spoken by the other. Wordsworth, of course, told us as much in his 'Preface' to the *Lyrical Ballads*: 'a poet is a man speaking to men', but he is a man who is

> endowed with more lively sensibility, more enthusiasm and tenderness, who has a greater knowledge of human nature and a more comprehensive soul, than are supposed to be common among mankind; a man pleased with his own passions and volitions, and who rejoices more than other men in the spirit of life that is in him; . . .[4]

Wordsworth is here stressing not only the individual voice, but also the strong individuality behind that individual voice, an individuality that marks out the poet as a man who is living his life more intensely, more alertly and feelingly, than others. And if we think back across the years since the Second World War, we can hear certain voices, individual and unmistakable, rising above the hubbub of ordinary voices, poetic or non-poetic. Philip Larkin's was one of them.

His voice was, fundamentally, very English. It is difficult to imagine him speaking another language, except in a very English

way, like Winston Churchill or Ernest Bevin. His defiant
Englishness ('*Foreign* poetry? No!') was no doubt designed to
disturb the conventional pieties of cultural internationalism, but
the figure sitting on the road sign at Coldstream with the word
'ENGLAND' and the St George's Cross on it was deeply concerned,
not only with the sense of place, but also with the deeply English
use of words, the barely-noticed inflections, the use of idioms, the
curious turn of phrase, the way in which a certain tone of voice or
a way of putting something reveals the speaker's character:

> 'This was Mr Bleaney's room. He stayed
> The whole time he was at the Bodies, till
> They moved him.'
>
> > ('Mr Bleaney')

There is nothing particularly wrong with this, nothing ungramma-
tical, no solecism: yet the ear picks up a certain way of saying
things, perhaps the casual abbreviation of 'the Bodies' or of 'He
stayed/The whole time', something very slightly informal, not
quite as it should be between strangers. In this poem it contrasts,
of course, with the other voice, the poet's own, observant,
reflective, ultimately puzzled at the kind of life led by someone
like Mr Bleaney. Voices in Larkin are sometimes obviously brash
(though not obviously enough for some critics) as in 'Naturally
the Foundation', or as in the harsh tones of Jake Balokowsky, in
'Posterity':

> 'Christ, I just told you. Oh, you know the thing,
> That crummy textbook stuff from Freshman Psych,
> Not out of kicks or something happening –
> One of those old-type *natural* fouled-up guys.'

These are examples of a use of English that is obviously, perhaps
too obviously, coarsened: Larkin is not at his best when he is
beating hell out of the American postgraduate scene. His English
voice is better when he is using it subtly and carefully to reveal
character. We learn something in 'Livings', for instance, even
from a simple phrase like 'Father's dead' (although, of course, a
great deal of its effect depends on its context, on its relationship
with what surrounds it, so that the words 'Father's dead' are
given added meaning from the circumstantial detail which the

poem so effectively supplies). What sort of a man would reflect in quite these words, in just such a way? Conventional, yes; unrebellious, accepting; the opposite, one might say, of Meursault in *L'Étranger*: 'Aujourd'hui, maman est morte'. But where does this oppositeness come from? I would guess from a certain tone as well as context, a tone that is so deep as to be almost impenetrable. And what kind of a person would say, as the distinguished cousin of the mayor says in 'I Remember, I Remember',

> There
> *Before us, had we the gift to see ahead –*

There is nothing wrong with this as part of a sentence, nothing that a translator could not provide a straight equivalent for (as, indeed, Renato Oliva and Camillo Pennati have done):

> Di fronte a noi, se potessimo avere
> il dono di vedere nel futuro[5]

I wonder if this has quite the same resonance in Italian as it does in English, whether it reveals quite the same unmistakable self-satisfaction, quite the same air of benevolent and orotund banality. It contrasts, of course, with the other two voices in the poem, those of the friend and of the poet himself:

> 'You look as if you wished the place in Hell,'
> My friend said, 'judging from your face.' 'Oh well,
> I suppose it's not the place's fault,' I said.

This is the individual voice again, the authentic tone of a certain mood: 'Oh well' . . . 'I suppose' . . . 'It's not the place's fault'. The end of the poem can thus be both colloquial and epigrammatic:

> 'Nothing, like something, happens anywhere.'

This is a flourish, or rather an anti-flourish, a neat antithesis to end the poem with; it belongs in part to rhetoric, and it compresses so neatly what has gone before that it is easy to see it as a piece of consummate artistry. Yet it also belongs to the voice which has been talking across the railway carriage, reflecting on the changes from childhood to youth and from youth to middle age: it carries with it the almost unbearable accumulations of a past that was boring and ordinary. The line belongs partly to the faculty which sees in it a look back to Thomas Hood and the poem's title; but it belongs also to that voice of a poet who is setting up the poem to be an antitype of the usual poems about childhood:

'Was that,' my friend smiled, 'where you "have your roots"?'
No, only where my childhood was unspent,
I wanted to retort . . .

The pressures of authenticity swing the poem from Wordsworth towards Hardy, from the image of a childhood with roots in *The Prelude* ('Fair seed-time had my soul') to the use of 'un-' words in Hardy.[6] But beyond and alongside, if not beneath these literary echoes there is the tone, the barely perceptible alterations of mood which are felt through the speaker's voice, from the first surprise, 'Why, Coventry!' to the puzzlement at how it had changed, to the centre of the poem, the expansion of the word 'unspent'. In those verses, the poet plays with the clichés of childhood and adolescent experience: and yet the very poem itself is curiously triumphant, a making of something out of the very nothing which is proclaimed at the end.

The poem is almost an assertion of a voice, a voice of an individual with a past. It is that which was Larkin's great discovery through Hardy, sometime after the publication of *The North Ship*. *The North Ship* is full of other poets' voices, notably Celtic ones, such as Yeats and Dylan Thomas. *The Less Deceived* is a rejection of the Celtic voice, an adoption of a certain kind of English voice, a Midland one, a grammar-school and Oxford one, a voice whose tones are sometimes obvious, sometimes difficult to catch, but always individual: it is a voice which depends on Larkin's own accumulated experience, and in it we hear the poet's own history, issuing forth in what T. S. Eliot called 'the auditory imagination'. This is 'the feeling for syllable and rhythm, penetrating far below the conscious levels of thought and feeling'; it is quoted by Seamus Heaney at the beginning of his essay on 'Englands of the Mind', in which he contrasts Larkin's Englishness with the different Englishness of Ted Hughes and Geoffrey Hill. Heaney suggests that Eliot was thinking of what Heaney describes as

1 Assessing the progress of the new library, August 1958

2 Hot work! The move into the new library, September 1959

3 (*above*) One of the happiest occasions in the University's history. The official opening of the library by Her Majesty, Queen Elizabeth, the Queen Mother, June 1960 (the Chancellor of the University, Lord Middleton, is looking on)

4 (*left*) '[Days] are to be happy in': a study in tranquillity, September 1961

5 (above) Planning stage II of the library, June 1964

6 (right) At 39, a still youthful-looking Larkin, September 1961

7 (*above*) Philip Larkin with the poet Ted Hughes, at the University of Hull, May 1975.
(Ted Hughes was appointed Poet Laureate in December 1984)

8 (*below*) Philip Larkin chairing a talk given by Ted Hughes at the University of Hull, May 197!

9 (*above*) Three 'Hull' poets: Andrew Motion and Douglas Dunn with Philip Larkin outside the Brynmor Jones Library, November 1979

10 (*below*) Philip Larkin with Barry Bloomfield at the launching of his bibliography on Philip Larkin (1933–76), November 1979

11 (*above*) Librettist and composer (Anthony Hedges) discuss the score of *Bridge for the Living*, written to celebrate the opening of the Humber Bridge, March 1981

12 (*below*) Philip Larkin with Edwin A. Dawes and Dale Salwak after dinner and entertainment at Dawes' home, July 1982

13 (*above*) A humorous aside during the after-luncheon speech commemorating the 80th birthday of Sir Brynmor Jones (seated), October 1983

14 (*below*) Edwin A. Dawes (Chairman of the Library Committee), Sir Brynmor Jones (Vice Chancellor, University of Hull, 1956–72), Sir Roy Marshall (Vice Chancellor), and Philip Larkin (Librarian), at the celebration of Sir Brynmor's 80th birthday, October 1983

15 Philip Larkin with
Patti and Dale
Salwak, 27 July 1

16 Philip Larkin,
April 1984

the cultural depth-charge latent in certain words and rhythms, that binding secret between words in poetry that delights not just the ear but the whole backward and abysm of mind and body; thinking of the relationship between the words as pure vocable, as articulate noise, and the word as etymological occurrence, as symptom of human history, memory and attachments.[7]

In Philip Larkin's case, the voice, the way in which the poems are spoken, becomes (as it does with all poets, I suspect) inextricably and curiously entangled with the 'voice' which is heard through every reading, silent, hearing the poem through the inner ear, or aloud. In Larkin's poems it is unmistakably English in a particular way. The trick in 'Lines on a Young Lady's Photograph Album', for example, is to provide a special shifting of the voice which is associated with a characteristically English self-deprecation into another voice of admiration and love; indeed the two are made to interact in a way which is not easy to pin down or describe. The poem moves from the first caricature of the desperately curious young man, 'devouring' the pictures:

> Too much confectionery, too rich:
> I choke on such nutritious images.
>
> My swivel eye hungers from pose to pose . . .

The hints of the absurd are strong here: as in 'I Remember, I Remember', there is a stereotype around, here the callow youth: we pick up his greediness, his unseemly haste, through the comic vocabulary – 'confectionery', 'my swivel eye'. Behind this there is the voice of the poet himself, who is the callow youth yet who can see himself as such. He wryly contemplates his own voyeurism, turning it off with a laughing parenthesis about transvestism:

> Or lifting a heavy-headed rose
> Beneath a trellis, or in a trilby hat
>
> (Faintly disturbing, that, in several ways) –

The voice registers the degree of seriousness, or unseriousness: the ear and the mind together pick up the true line of the poem,

which moves from imbalance to balance: the first lines are full of
an unseemly gobbling (even to a 'choke') of the experience, which
gives way to another tone, in which the trilby hat is disturbing,
but only faintly so; if it is disturbing, we are made to see, it is
because the speaker is robustly 'normal', suspicious of anything
that might be associated with transvestism. To glance at such a
serious subject is to invite the laughter which comes from
incongruity, and the raised eyebrow is clearly detectable in the
tone which follows:

> From every side you strike at my control,
> Not least through these disquieting chaps who loll
> At ease about your earlier days:
> Not quite your class, I'd say, dear, on the whole.

The last line is patronising in an attempt to clear away the
'disquieting chaps'; the uneasiness is obvious, and so is the
comedy. Its use of cliché – 'not quite your class' – and the dreadful
intimacy of 'dear' are intended as part of the comic vision. Yet
that comic vision is not totally reductive. It is found, to be sure, in
the mock-heroic 'But o, photography!', which modulates into
double-edged reflection ('faithful and disappointing'), but it then
accommodates another voice

> what grace
> Your candour thus confers upon her face!

'Grace' here is a magic word, one which allows the voice of the
poem to include not only a certain self-deprecating amusement,
but also to convey a true sense of admiration, almost of a courtly
love. But then the tone changes again:

> So I am left
> To mourn (without a chance of consequence)
> You, balanced on a bike against a fence;
> To wonder if you'd spot the theft
> Of this one of you bathing;

The mood changes with mercurial swiftness here, from the
mourning at the irrecoverable past to the cheeky and venturesome
present. In Philip Larkin's reading of this poem, there is just the

slightest pause before 'bathing', and the slightest emphasis on it, just to make clear the comic vision of the speaker in possession of a picture of his girlfriend in a bathing costume. But then, as though it has had enough of this fooling, the voice reaches towards a final equilibrium

> and you lie
> Unvariably lovely there,
> Smaller and clearer as the years go by.

It is, I think, the ability to render such complex mixtures of seriousness and unseriousness, that mixture of comic inadequacy, wry self-understanding, and sadness for the time that has past, that makes this poem so unusual. Any attempt to read it requires a sensitivity to tone, to degrees of seriousness or unseriousness, which is difficult to teach and which probably has to be apprehended instinctively, through the mind and body (and perhaps by a native speaker of English only). And when we add to these constituents the final one, the grace and charm that touches everyone through love and the declaration of love, the poem becomes a difficult exercise in complex familiarities. It is difficult, not because of the ideas or the language, but because it is necessary to get the voice right: it is necessary to understand, too, that this voice can be both funny and serious, can allow an interaction of the two which is almost simultaneous. I think of this, perhaps arbitrarily and too exclusively, as an English trait; it is part of some process in Philip Larkin's poetry which goes very deep, so that the figure on the ENGLAND sign is only an emblem of something powerful and hidden, seen only by glimpses. Oddly enough (in the context of Philip Larkin's poetry) the best expression of what I am trying to describe is by Roland Barthes:

A language is . . . on the hither side of literature. Style is almost beyond it: imagery, delivery, vocabulary spring from the body and past of the writer and gradually become the very reflexes of his art. Thus under the name of style a self-suffucient language is evolved which has its roots only in the depths of the author's personal and secret mythology, that sub-nature of expression where the first coition of words and things takes place, where once and for all the great verbal themes of his existence come to be installed.[8]

By the Englishness of Philip Larkin's writing I mean what Barthes
has identified here, the way in which imagery, delivery and
vocabulary spring 'from the body and past of the writer'.
Consequently an awareness of what might be involved in that
body and that past is one reason for emphasising Philip Larkin's
particular use of English. Its familiarity with the subtle nuances of
spoken English allows such pyrotechnic effects as the verse in
'Toads':

> Ah, were I courageous enough
>   To shout *Stuff your pension!*
> But I know, all too well, that's the stuff
>   That dreams are made on:

The subjunctive reveals the remoteness of the possibility: yet the
shout itself is comic, and so is the importation of Prospero's
phrase from *The Tempest*. The verse is delicately balanced between
comedy and tragedy, between light-heartedness and seriousness,
waiting for the resolution at the end of the poem. Indeed, one of
the most effective elements of a Larkin poem is the setting up of a
trembling instability, a delicate balance, which is gently but firmly
resolved at the end of the poem; and the resolution is often a
matter of deciding which voice in the end is going to predominate.
Here there is a comic form, with its rhymes 'enough/stuff' and
'pension/made on', enclosing an underlying seriousness and
longing.

II

The voice, or voices, then, are extremely important in Philip
Larkin's poetry. To them we should add his own voice, his way
of speaking and writing: as Barthes noted, 'imagery, delivery,
vocabulary spring from the body and past of the writer', and one
of the themes of the present essay is delivery – in this case the
spoken voice – as well as the 'voice' in its more customary
metonymic sense of 'the poet's voice'.[9] I have said that Philip had
a good voice, and an English voice: it was a good voice, too, in
that it spoke and wrote good English: when Philip used the
English language, he did so with a kind of instinctive respect for
its ability to express things with clarity and feeling. He had a sure

ear for the misuse of the language, from the churchman's 'heah endeth' (guyed in the reading of 'Church Going') to the children's 'Mam, get us one of them to keep' ('Take One Home for the Kiddies'). The thoughtless cruelty to animals, which so distressed Philip, is here associated with a coarseness of speech – no 'please' or 'thank you', no shape or grace to the expression. In contrast there is in *Required Writing* hardly a sentence that could have been better put: the prose is informative, to the point, clean. Philip Larkin spoke the Queen's English properly, and he would have thought it affected, and perhaps disloyal, to be sloppy or careless: when he received the Shakespeare Prize in Hamburg in 1976 he spoke of his predecessor, John Masefield, as 'a writer whose strength and simplicity I have long admired'.[10] His own strength and simplicity in reviews and other short pieces are admirable. Yet he was not stuffy: he was not above using colloquialisms where necessary, and he could introduce a lively informality when required. He was, like a number of his contemporaries (see the introduction to *Jill*) a good mimic, and his prose was always lively and never stiff and starchy. He knew, and relished the flexibility of English, just as he loved the variety and flexibility of its writers, from Shakespeare to Evelyn Waugh and Thomas Hardy. For him, the English language was a very precious thing, and his speaking and writing of it were good because he had so much respect for it. He would not, I think, have seen himself as doing anything as grand as purifying the dialect of the tribe, but he knew that in the proper use of words he was at least playing his part in keeping clean and healthy the language that he loved. He was immediately sensitive to bad usage (see the review entitled 'The Batman from Blades' in *Required Writing*), and for him bad usage was, I believe, allied to bad character. It could be found in the worst kind of on-the-make exploitation of the academic system:

You've got to work at this: after all, you don't expect to understand anything as important as art straight off, do you? I mean, this is pretty complex stuff: if you want to know how complex, I'm giving a course of ninety-six lectures at the local college, starting next week, and you'd be more than welcome. The whole thing's on the rates, you won't have to pay. After all, think what asses people have made of themselves in the past by not understanding art – you don't want to be like that, do you?[11]

Clearly Larkin has here invented a caricature of a deliberate and callous cultural bullying, but this is signified also by its particularly nauseous use of the English language ('pretty complex stuff . . . you'd be more than welcome . . . you don't want to be like that'). For Philip Larkin, in other words, the English language was part of a scheme of values. He did not believe in sloppy abbreviations or modish modernisms – 'yeah', 'dunno', 'innit'; rather he used words properly, as a craftsman should. He always admired things that were done well, with skill and patience, and with respect for the materials. He recognised the craft in 'Show Saturday' instinctively:

> blanch leeks like church candles, six pods of
> Broad beans (one split open), dark shining-leafed cabbages –
>   rows
> Of single supreme versions, followed (on laced
> Paper mats) by dairy and kitchen; four brown eggs, four white
>   eggs,
> Four plain scones, four dropped scones, pure excellences that
>   enclose
> A recession of skills.

These are examples of a proper perfection, of something done properly, with respect for the materials and with acquired skill and practice. Such exhibits are works of art, testimonies to the dedication of their makers, and in the same way the poems are witnesses to a careful, respectful, almost tender use of the English language, a usage that comes from love.

III

Philip Larkin's poems often appear to be like the exhibits in the show, 'pure excellences that enclose/A recession of skills'. The images are held in them as clearly as Chardin or Cézanne might have seen them; and they have in some ways a certain formality, an unusual (for these days) firmness of form, a considered arrangement of verse and line, an organisation of type on the white page which emphasises their air of permanence and solidity. Yet as a Chinese jar, in Eliot's phrase, 'moves perpetually in its stillness', so Philip Larkin's poems have that quality of living and breathing life which comes from the voice, the delivery, and with it the sense of the original felt idea. The poems move in the stillness through the voice, with its ever-changing and marvellous flexibility, its subtle movement of tone, its proper poetic dignity holding within itself a deep capacity for feeling, but also a certain individuality and impenetrable force. The most obvious place to find this is in the recordings which Philip Larkin made of his three volumes, one recording for each decade from the 1950s to the 1970s. He was very interested in the possibilities of such recordings, although he did not think that he read his own poems particularly well (wrongly, most listeners will feel). He discussed the subject of reading, briefly, in his review of Francis Berry's *Poetry and the Physical Voice* when it came out in 1962, recording his antiquarian rage at 'legions of pre-1928 tenors and sopranos we preserved when nobody thought to record, say, Hardy or Lawrence'.[12] He noted with some curiosity that he allowed Eliot's reading of 'Prufrock' to go on to the very end, and he was clearly fascinated by Francis Berry's theories about the shrillness of Shelley's voice or the deepening of Milton's.

His own voice was, as I have said, a good one. It was a fine, manly bass, with a higher register which co-existed with the depth, like an octave note (it seems to me to have been naturally pitched somewhere around a low G – the open-string G of a cello – with a simultaneous pitch one octave higher). Its range was considerable, and listening carefully to the record there is a surprising amount of variation of pitch, tone, speed and expression. This occurs, of course, in the counterpoint of 'voices' which has already been referred to, between Mr Bleaney's landlady (for example) and the poet-lodger. But it occurs also in 'single-voiced' poems, often in the co-presence within the poem of different moods and swings of tone. A poem such as 'Toads', for instance, begins with a kind of jaunty insecurity which is rendered in Philip Larkin's reading by a high note on the opening 'Why' (italics mine):

> *Why* should I let the toad *work*
> Squat on my life?

This high note recurs in the first part of the poem:

> Six days of the *week* . . .
> *Just* for *paying* a *few bills*!

The voice deepens in pitch in the second part of the poem, as it often does in Larkin's poetry, although one of the effects of the recording of this particular poem is that the reading emphasises the humour of the poem rather than its underlying seriousness. Words such as '*Lecturers*' are very slightly emphasised, held up for inspection for a moment with wry amusement, along with

> *Lots* of folk live up *lanes*
> With *fires* in a bucket . . .
>
> Their nippers have got *bare feet* . . .

The emphasis is slight, but quite perceptible. Sometimes it alters the feel of a line, as in

> something sufficiently toad-like
> Squats in me, too; . . .

where I think the natural way of reading would be '*Squats* in *me*, too', but where the poet's reading is firmly 'Squats *in* me, too'. But whatever the choice of stress, the interesting thing is that the early lightness, the high pitch in places, is succeeded by a more regular and less disturbed pitch, as though the poem is settling down to a certain stability, an appropriate reflection rather than an amused description. The same pattern is observable in 'Church Going', although here the reflective voice tends to dominate. In the early part of the poem, however, there are occasional flashes of higher pitch and stronger emphasis:

> *Hatless*, I take off
> My *cycle*-clips . . .

And there is the mimicry, already mentioned, of 'heah endeth'. On the whole, however, even the early part of the reading is marked by a certain rather passionate monotone, not unlike that of T. S. Eliot:

I sign the book, donate an Irish sixpence,
Reflect the place was not worth stopping for.

Yet stop I did: in fact I often do,
And always end much at a loss like this,
Wondering what to look for; . . .

This is a very good example of the way in which the tone and
pitch of voice can govern a reading and interpretation. At this
point there is no attempt to make something funny out of the
Irish sixpence; it becomes part of a certain regular and reflective
tone, a kind of baffled and agnostic weariness that the reading
brings out. This is, of course, succeeded by something else:

A serious house on serious earth it is,
In whose blent air all our compulsions meet,
Are recognised, and robed as destinies . . .

Here the deep tone that has been present throughout acquires a
new sustained resonance. In earlier verses there were moments of
resolute depth:

Bored, unin*formed* . . .

but in the last verse it is as though new notes have been added to
enrich the poem's consistent bass. In the reading, the word
'serious' is given just that slight emphasis, to show that out of all
the words which he might have chosen, out of all the words the
poem has been slowly working towards, he has finally lighted
upon the word 'serious' as the *right* word, the one which holds
most completely the meaning of the place which he has been
trying to express.

The most common movement in *The Less Deceived* is from this
initial liveliness of description, expressed in a widening voice
register, to a consequential reflection, in which the voice stabilises.
However, the last poem in the collection, 'At Grass', does not
follow this pattern. It is much more evenly read: it becomes a
poem which is incapable of the usual jokiness because the
predominating emotion, and the emotion which the poet is most
concerned to bring out, is that of love. He watches the beautiful
horses enjoying the simplicity of their retirement, their fame now

gone; he has no room for anything except an intent concentration on their lives, and, beyond that, the sense of transience and the passing of all things. In many ways it is the boldest poem in *The Less Deceived*, the one in which the poet is most vulnerable because of this uninhibited use of sentiment. The reading makes no concessions: anyone looking for irony, that most useful of defences, will have to look elsewhere. It is a poem which is moving because of its unflinching simplicity, in which

> Only the groom, and the groom's boy,
> With bridles in the evening come.

The sentiment comes with the close of day: these horses are in the evening of their lives, and their simple pleasures of eating grass or galloping 'for what must be joy' are a way – a good way – of spending their last years. And behind this picture is the sense of time itself, that procession of faded, classic Junes that are no longer present but past, recorded in almanacs but gone for ever. The voice registers this by an absolute evenness, a rigorous intensity of expression which conveys to the listener a quality which is present in the printed text but which is now fully brought out.

In reviewing Francis Berry's book, Philip Larkin noted the interesting idea that Milton's voice changed. It dropped in pitch, and the voice of *Paradise Lost* shows that 'his temperament has become graver, [and] so has his vocal organ'.[13] Philip's own voice changed and deepened in a rather similar way. It was still capable of variety and mimicry in *The Whitsun Weddings*, as in 'Toads Revisited' with its bouncy high-pitched imitation of the secretarial 'shall-I-keep-the-call-in-Sir'; but at the end of that poem it slows and settles in to the even-toned resignation of

> Give me your arm, old toad;
> Help me down Cemetery Road.

We can become aware at this point that the poet's reading is a realisation of mood: in this case it is a subtle mixture of pain and wry amusement, a plea of something (in this case work) to help to make life bearable and to give it shape and purpose. Together with this there is the affectionate grin at the self, attached to the strange work/toad creature, walking arm-in-arm towards death. It is a very good example of a certain figurative element in metaphor which is part of the complex process of imaginative apprehension:[14] in this case it gives a certain comic turn to the poignant realisation that getting on with our work is the best thing we can do, a *Candide*-like acceptance of the ultimate elusiveness of the ideal. The inevitability of death, so lightly touched here, occurs elsewhere in *The Whitsun Weddings* with a very different tone of voice attached:

> Life is first boredom, then fear.
> Whether or not we use it, it goes,
> And leaves what something hidden from us chose,
> And age, and then the only end of age.
>
> ('Dockery and Son')

This sense of death has appeared before, in 'Next Please', with its final image of the black-sailed ship: but in *The Whitsun Weddings* the tone deepens and steadies, becomes more grave, becomes weightier. Even 'The Whitsun Weddings' itself, that central poem in the collection, is marked by a certain steady gravity, a compassionate observation rather than a self-satisfied superiority. The poet is on his train journey, and the newlyweds are on theirs: he is together with them on the train in 'this frail/Travelling coincidence', but in every other respect he is poles apart from them, so that the poem becomes a meditation on togetherness and separateness. For the young married couples, the journey is a momentous moment, their first time together as Mr and Mrs, one of those extraordinary moments (perhaps *the* most extraordinary moment) of significant change in human life. In his reading of this poem, Philip Larkin assumed, not the throwaway tones of the opening of 'Church Going', but a certain rather serious correctness, so that the description of the send-off parties is taken absolutely straight:

> the perms,
> The nylon gloves and jewellery-substitutes,
> The lemons, mauves, and olive-ochres that
>
> Marked off the girls unreally from the rest.

It is the straightness of tone, the absence of any flicker of amusement, that saves this passage from becoming patronising. Indeed, if 'The Whitsun Weddings' is read with the voice of *The Less Deceived*, a kind of disaster occurs, a profoundly mistaken hilarity; in many places, a youthful high-spiritedness has been superseded by a finer tone, an aching sensitiveness to the passing of time and the failure of human aspiration. So the corresponding opening poem to 'Lines on a Young Lady's Photograph Album' is now 'Here', that open-eyed description of the approaches to Hull, of the city itself, and of the East Riding beyond. Instead of the close intimacy of the heads bent together over the album there is now the detachment of the observer of the Saturday shoppers and the poet who is aware of the fields and the air beyond, and of the sea beyond that:

> Here is unfenced existence:
> Facing the sun, untalkative, out of reach.

The poem is aiming further now, his grave observation stretching beyond the town, out to sea, out into the space that is beyond farmland and beach, out into the endless other of the sky and air.

Milton's voice became deeper: the resonances of *Paradise Lost* are different from what Francis Berry calls the 'sharp and plangent' – though musical and tuneable – voice of the earlier years.[15] Philip Larkin's voice also changed and became deeper, and it can be seen to have done so in *High Windows*. It occurs most obviously, perhaps, in the image of depth itself:

> Man hands on misery to man.
> It deepens like a coastal shelf.
> ('This be the Verse')

The image is so powerful here that it does not need an emphasis in the reading, and does not receive one; but its presence in this poem is part of the acknowledgement in *High Windows* that in some way, whatever you do, the cards are stacked against you. What distinguishes *High Windows* is the sense, as Ronald Draper has finely put it, that Philip Larkin is 'the most contemporary of our contemporaries in his straightforward acceptance that this is the only life we have, and that we cannot escape the tormenting consciousness of its "only end"'.[16] This emerges clearly enough in the reading of these poems: what can be discerned is a dignity and firmness of the voice, something quite unlike the playfulness of earlier poems. It is as though the poet, as he reads some of these examples of lyric tragedy (to borrow Professor Draper's term) is gritting his teeth and determining to go through with the process of living. His voice has a clipped and even precise quality about it in places, indicating a kind of determination: these poems are intent on 'telling the truth about life as it is'.[17] Yet beside the facing-out of despair, there are many other things: the reading of 'Dublinesque', for example, is a revelation of the poet's joy at perceiving something which is pathetic and yet strangely beautiful. He reads the poem in a kind of 'surprised by joy' voice which is evidence of something extremely important in *High Windows*: the readiness to be surprised by the endless variety, beauty and oddity of life. The sense of accumulated living is one of the strongest elements in the volume: all those different, disparate lives, the commercial traveller in 1929, the ancient college fellows, the card-players, the families at the seaside, the emigrant; and, in addition, all those deaths – not only the miners in 'The Explosion' but the people in hospital, and the geriatrics in 'The Old Fools'.

The voice which gives expression to this is clearly different from the voice of *The Less Deceived* and *The Whitsun Weddings*. It could be said, I think, that there was a Larkin voice for each decade and for each book: 1955, 1964, 1974. Certainly that was how it felt, I know, for some of the poet's readers (and listeners to the recordings), for whom each volume contained a particular 'voice' for that time and that place.

The voice of *High Windows* is a voice of an accumulated experience. It has lost any uncertainty of tone, and some of the earlier taste for mimicry, although that remains where necessary, as in the opening of 'Vers de Société'. In the reading, the voice of the inviter is given as a shrill falsetto, to emphasise a certain tiresomeness which is nevertheless, as the poem brilliantly discovers, preferable to remaining at home. What is noticeable about the reading of this poem is the way in which certain words are given emphasis to bring out the latent and indeterminate meanings: a phrase such as (italics mine)

Something that bores us, something we don't *do well*

is taken quite slowly, allowing the listener to explore the sub-text of the poem, the spaces between the words, and the polysemic properties of them. Indeed, one of the features of the recording of *High Windows* is the way in which the reading is slower than before. It is the voice of reflection, but also of a discovered, an earned authority:

> It may be that through habit these do best,
> Coming to water clumsily undressed
> Yearly; teaching their children by a sort
> Of clowning; helping the old, too, as they ought.
>   ('To the Sea')

As they ought; so they should. In the same voice of authority the poet blesses another yearly ritual, the annual show;

> Let it stay hidden there like strength, below
> Sale-bills and swindling;
>
>   .   .   .
>
>   something they share
> That breaks ancestrally each year into
> Regenerate union. Let it always be there.
>   ('Show Saturday')

Such endings make it very clear where the poet stands, and so does a poem such as 'Homage to a Government'. There is, in other words, a new firmness of purpose (it comes out in the firmness of the reading) and a voice which is not only lyric and tragic but also encouraging and admonitory. It can observe life as livings and dyings, as hopes and failures, but also as containing wonderfully precious moments – the spring, with the trees 'in fullgrown thickness every May' or the voice in the Dublin street

> heard singing
> Of Kitty, or Katy,
> As if the name meant once
> All love, all beauty.
>   ('Dublinesque')

The precious fragile moment is here inextricably linked to the sense of sadness which accompanies the funeral: the force of 'once' is understated, and almost unbearably poignant because of its unobtrusive strength.

The range of *High Windows* is thus extraordinary, from the controlled and deep seriousness of a poem such as 'The Building', to the desperation of 'The Old Fools', the self-deprecation of 'Annus Mirabilis', and the compassionate observation of 'To the Sea'. What is interesting, in hearing the recording of Philip Larkin reading these poems, is how they all seem to be very various and yet inescapably his: there is no loss of integrity in placing such widely different poems together. The preservation of this integrity is a result, I think, of the sense that, however various, these poems spring, in Barthes's phrase, 'from the body and the past of the writer'.[18] It generates a sense of a peculiar honesty, so that the reader can believe that Philip Larkin would (and indeed did) speak these lines from the heart. It is a trick, if it can be called such, that he caught from Hardy, whose work has the same kind of blend of severity and wry laughter, the same rich counterpoint of irony and straight talking. And what is true of *High Windows* is true of all Philip Larkin's poetry. The voice which reads the poems from 1955 to 1974 is recognisably that of one person, however much it may be seen to have changed.

It is the variety of this 'voice', and of the physical voice that I would end by insisting on. Philip Larkin did not write light verse as such, although he commented in one of the recordings that 'Naturally the Foundation' had been seen as light verse (he suggested that it was straight description, but this was, I think, disingenuous). What the readings of these poems do is to indicate when the poetry is to be taken straight; and at other times to offer up, very gently, the possibility of taking the poem's statements with a pinch of salt, or of seeing the poem's subjects and treatment (which are inseparable) as ever so slightly ridiculous. Philip Larkin was too sensitive a poet to bash the reader, and there is no sense of 'laugh, or else . . .' that is sometimes found in light verse; but the opportunity is there. It is given by the turn of the voice towards, not the ridiculous, but the possibility of the ridiculous. The result is the aural equivalent of the raised eyebrow, the quizzical look, the twitch at the corner of the mouth, the twinkle in the eye. These signs are found in the slight pause, the lift of the voice, the occasional emphasis.

At the other extreme there is the deepening of tone, the concentrated intensity, and the ground-bases of solemnity and seriousness. Between the two, of course, are the immense ranges of feeling and apprehension. As Barbara Everett has pointed out in a brilliant essay, Philip Larkin's poetry is in no way simple. He said, she points out, that his poems are too simple to profit from criticism; but she then goes on to point out that simple is an awkward term:

> to believe without reservations in the simplicity of Larkin's work is another matter – except in so far as an artistry is a simplification of life, an abnormally clear noticing of human conditions that come to the rest of us fogged with the general imprecisions of the usual. To this degree, all good writing is magnificently simple. But it is unsafe for anyone other than its writer to say so. For the simple gets confused with quite different things – with the literal; with the crude; with the artless and sociological.[19]

I agree with her reading of Larkin so wholeheartedly that the present essay may be seen only as trying to do the same thing – to point out the complexity and richness of feeling and treatment in his work. I have tried to suggest that this is found, quite naturally, in the 'voices' of the poems, and in the tone of voice with which Philip Larkin read them. The two things, of course, interact, sometimes in a complementary way and sometimes with surprise. And in this there is an ultimate elusiveness. In a rather simple sense we can see that Philip Larkin's readings of the poetry provides a kind of 'interpretation' of them, but in a more subtle sense these readings take the poems off the page and give them back to the poet's private self, back to the body and past of the writer. It is the opposite of the freeing of the word by placing it as a legible text on the page, for the reader to establish his own indeterminate relationship with it. It is a reminder that the poet has his own claim to his own poems. His physical voice asserts his poetic voice, and (to some degree) stands against interference.

I should like to illustrate this by a final anecdote, against myself. In 1975, not long after the publication of *High Windows*, I wrote an article about Philip's poetry.[20] At the time he was having a rather bad run with the critics, and I was attempting to defend him from charges of being just a whining commentator on the England of the 1970s. I identified a strain in his poetry of what I can only call 'religious' thought, which seemed to me to have gone unnoticed and to suggest that he was a more serious poet than most people had perceived. I now think the article overstated the case, but at the time it seemed a good idea. I knew Philip slightly, well enough to send him a copy; and I was seeing him quite frequently in those days during his weekend visits to Leicester and Loughborough. I waited for some reaction to the article; none came. I went on waiting: still nothing. Then on about the third or fourth occasion, he said with profound gloom: 'Thank you for writing about me; it made me sound very deep.' As he said the words his voice went down and down, into the depths of some central reservoir of himself where he kept all sorts of things which he found tiresome, or painful, or sad, or maybe just a bit of a nuisance. By the time he got to the word 'deep' it was somewhere in the region of his lowest bass register, a low F or E. I had become for a moment (we remained friends) one of the army of nuisances that swarmed about him (in spite of his best efforts to keep them at arm's length). Unless, of course (and this would be quite possible) he was pulling my leg. I shall never know.

11

Tentative Initiation in the Poetry[*]

John H. Augustine

A recent article in *Commentary* by Joseph Epstein entitled 'Miss Pym and Mr Larkin' discusses the importance of isolation to the poetry of Philip Larkin. 'A stammerer as a boy, increasingly deaf in middle age – Larkin's life neatly conspired to set him apart and keep him there', writes Epstein. 'What is impressive', he continues, 'is the way that he was able to generalize his own apartness into persuasive poems about the isolation, the loneliness that is part of the condition of us all.'[1] Larkin does not simply make himself into a case study. Epstein's attention to what he calls, variously, Larkin's 'spiritual' or 'radical' isolation echoes other critics' emphasis on this theme. Bruce Martin also sees it as central to Larkin's work: 'loneliness, or at least the sense of being left out, colors almost all of Larkin's speakers and their personal situations.'[2] Correspondingly, this sense of exclusion stresses the importance of social experience in Larkin's poetry. Thus Larkin separates society and solitude as opposites. But in doing so, he describes a static state of tension with reference to a traditional process of initiation. In moving from solitude to integration into society, Larkin's protagonists often become stuck in the middle. Larkin describes stasis and paralysis. But he does so with reference to a pattern of movement. Initiation proceeds from isolation to integration: the loneliness which his protagonists feel comes in part from being unable to complete this transition. And it is this frustration which he polarises into opposites.

Initiation is a process by which the initiate gains knowledge of self, evil and of the world in general. Such an understanding is usually precipitated by an existential crisis or series of conflicts,

* For the writing of this essay I am indebted to the Graduate School of the University of Minnesota and the support of a Doctoral Dissertation Fellowship. A shorter version of this essay was presented at the 1986 Modern Language Association in New York City.

and is often accompanied by a sense of the loss of innocence and a strong sense of isolation. The term implies a progression and thus the purpose of successful initiation is usually integration into society. This process, however, can be interrupted or modified. Mordecai Marcus divides initiations into three types – tentative, uncompleted, and decisive:

> [First, some initiations lead] only to the threshold of maturity and understanding but do not definitely cross it. Such stories emphasize the shocking effect of experience, and their protagonists tend to be distinctly young. Second, some initiations take their protagonists across a threshold of maturity and understanding but leave them enmeshed in a struggle for certainty. These initiations sometimes involve self-discovery. Third, the most decisive initiations carry their protagonists firmly into maturity and understanding, or at least show them decisively embarked toward maturity. These initiations usually center on self-discovery.[3]

While Larkin's comments describing his youth as a 'forgotten boredom' in 'Coming' might suggest otherwise, his poetry reflects elements of all three types of initiation experiences – though the society-solitude tension described earlier insures that most examples fall in the uncompleted or tentative category. The tension of this incompletion forms the basis for several of Larkin's poems.

The poem 'Wires' in Larkin's volume *The Less Deceived* provides a paradigm for this process of initiation. It contains the essential elements of the uncompleted initiation experience, for though the 'Young steers become old cattle from that day', the poem's emphasis is on the harsh experience itself and many of the steers' problems, particularly the desire to be apart, 'Beyond the wires', remain. The first steps, however, have taken place and the young initiate appears, early in the poem, to be moving from the 'purer water' of illusion to the confining limits of reality.

Like the young steers, who – 'always scenting purer water' – find their expectations dashed by the limiting confines of electric fences, so the rhyme scheme in the first stanza – ABCD, apparently free to wander – also finds itself confined and ordered by the second stanza's inverse, but matching rhymes – DCBA. The resulting envelope structure, with its orderly link between stanzas, establishes a rhythmic boundary or fence for the young steers as well. The abruptness of this limitation is most apparent in line four, the final line of the first stanza. The line ends with the excessive or hopeful phrase, 'Beyond the wires', which suggests a youthful expectation for 'purer water', and points the reader outside the confines of the fence. The next stanza begins with the line, 'Leads them to blunder up against the wires'. The immediate, matching rhyme in line five puts an abrupt end to the hope of escaping limitations. Nevertheless, the poem's final phrase reflects another similar struggle. 'Their widest sense' again points the steers outside the limits of the electric fence – 'Beyond the wires' – only to impose a rhyme scheme linking the phrase to the opening reference to electric fences. Even the repetition of the word 'widest' in 'widest senses' of line one and line eight, while pursuing the boundaries of both sound and sense, leaves the young steers confined within their society, for no matter how wide and open the prairie, the electric fence still encloses it.

The animals are jolted into recognising limits when they 'blunder up against the wires/Whose muscle-shredding violence gives no quarter'. Loss of confidence through fear characterises the young steers as they discover limits through pain. Experience over time, however, seems to teach them that, like the old cattle, they face the limitations of reality as well.

Yet initiation is not a simple matter of either accepting or rejecting adult values or reality. It is a complicated process of what Jung calls 'individuation' involving, among other things, the trials of experience, a loss of innocence and childhood illusions, isolation, disillusion and uncertainty. In short, it is a complex process where the individual passes from innocence to knowledge and takes at least a tentative step toward maturity. Life becomes more and more a matter of what experience reveals and less and less of what imagination or fantasy creates. For Larkin, the process of development or initiation is linked with a conflict between optimistic expectations for the future and harsh experience in the present.

A central requirement for any initiation experience is a fall from innocence. One is most deceived in youth, before what Larkin calls the 'hail/Of occurrence' in 'Send No Money' teaches its bitter lessons. He mocks the assumption that experience will be fruitful and free from suffering. As Larkin notes in 'Next Please', it is possible to assume a future filled with happiness simply because time moves forward:

> Always too eager for future, we
> Pick up bad habits of expectancy.
> Something is always approaching; every day
> *Till then* we say.

Yet the speaker – and the reader with him – learns that, instead of fulfilment, the future's ultimate approach is a foreboding ship of death. Minor disappointments and missed opportunities culminate in a vague sense of wasted lives in 'Afternoons', a poem describing working-class mothers. Wedding dreams have been replaced by the fantasies of television. Larkin depicts the loss of hope and the dwindling of expectations for these women. Experience in society, like the unstable wind in 'Afternoons', has 'ruined' their symbols of more pleasant times.

Contemporary social references abound in Larkin's poetry. One function of these illusions is to describe the society that confronts the speaker during this process of initiation. These social forces lead to doubts and questions as the speaker realises that hopeful notions about an orderly world have little place in reality. This is true for the present as well as the past and future. The poem 'Triple Time' casts the present as a 'time traditionally soured, / A time unrecommended by event'. Ageing looms large as a subject in Larkin's work. The trials and dissatisfaction of experience over time often lead to a sense of disillusionment over the discarded dreams of youth. The resulting frustration is immense. Consequently, many of Larkin's poems exhibit lives filled with a sense of hopeless passivity rather than purposeful activity. The desire to escape the harsh experiences of time through immersion in society and to seek solitude through an escape from society's routines is accompanied by an equally strong fear of isolation.

The 'wish to be alone', however, may reflect a deeper 'desire of oblivion' on the order of a Freudian deathwish described in the poem 'Wants'. This desire persists despite the allure of 'invitation-cards', the 'printed directions of sex', the 'tabled fertility rites', 'life insurance', and the family 'photographed under the flagstaff'. Each item described is one step removed from a decisive initiation into society or personal relationships. They are stylised representations of what is supposed to connect. But for the unsuccessful or tentative initiate, there is little choice but to opt for some kind of artificial alternative in an attempt to escape from the mundane and forget one's isolation. Thus the couple whose wedding album sits vacantly on the television set in 'Afternoons' now watch the BBC rather than relate to each other.

Isolation and initiation are not mutually exclusive. A particular period of isolation is, in fact, a central element of the initiation motif. While the fully initiated individual feels a sense of isolation due to the recognition of a clearer sense of self apart from others, the so-called 'tentatively initiated' individual – still mired in unresolved doubts and questions – faces another kind of isolation or loneliness from not having been integrated into adult society.

The poem 'Places, Loved Ones' speaks from the point of view of such a person, one who feels apart from society in a way which fails to define him. The speaker has found neither wife nor 'proper ground' and tries to defend and to justify his single state by devaluing marriage:

> To find such seems to prove
> You want no choice in where
> To build, or whom to love.
> You ask them to bear
> You off irrevocably,
> So that it's not your fault
> Should the town turn dreary,
> The girl a dolt.

Another characteristic of the Larkin initiate, and the final one I will mention here, is the speaker's self-conscious – and self-confessed – uncertainty about his definite choice to remain alone. The speaker betrays such ambivalence in 'Reasons for Attendance', where he takes the classic pose of an observer, rather than a participant. He stands outside and watches the dancers inside. In order to justify his decision not to join the crowd, he posits that the source of happiness depends on the individual. As in 'Places, Loved Ones', he devalues the sense of community which others have achieved. Others find happiness in couples, while he experiences happiness alone and in relation to art.

While the speaker appears to be absolutely definite about his choice and its consequences, he qualifies the entire argument in the last line of the poem:

> Therefore I stay outside,
> Believing this; and they maul to and fro,

> Believing that; and both are satisfied,
> If no one has misjudged himself. Or lied.

By acknowledging the possibility of self-deception, he includes himself among the potential self-deceivers.

Admittedly, Larkin's poetry does not portray a typical re-enactment of the familiar mythic archetype of the young hero who undertakes a dangerous journey that will initiate him into adulthood. Much of Larkin's work, however, does utilise important aspects of this motif, and a recognition of its central characteristics in the poetry reveals a dialectic between radical isolation and harsh experience – a desire for separation from society and a concurrent desire for integration into society. Larkin's protagonists have figuratively jolted against the wires of experience and come away shaken.

12

Philip Larkin: the Metonymic Muse[1]

David Lodge

1930s writing was, characteristically, antimodernist, realistic, readerly and metonymic. In the 1940s the pendulum of literary fashion swung back again – not fully, but to a perceptible degree – towards the pole we have designated as modernist, symbolist, writerly and metaphoric. Sooner or later the leading writers of the 1930s became disillusioned with politics, lost faith in Soviet Russia, took up religion, emigrated to America and fell silent. Christianity, in a very uncompromising, antihumanist, theologically 'high' form, became a force in literature (the later Eliot, the Charles Williams–C. S. Lewis circle, the 'Catholic novel' of Greene and Waugh). Bourgeois writers no longer felt obliged to identify with the proletariat. Bohemian, patrician, cosmopolitan attitudes and life-styles became once more acceptable in the literary world. To say that the English novel resumed experimentalism would be an overstatement; but 'fine writing' certainly returned and an interest in rendering the refinements of individual sensibility rather than collective experience. There was a revival of Henry James, and many people saw Charles Morgan as his modern successor. Fantasy, such as Upward and Isherwood had felt obliged to purge from their work, was luxuriated in by Mervyn Peake. There was great excitement at an apparent revival of verse drama, principally in the work of T. S. Eliot and Christopher Fry. Perhaps the movement of the pendulum was most evident in the field of poetry. The reputations of Eliot and Yeats triumphantly survived the attacks launched against them in the 1930s, and the most enthusiastically acclaimed younger poet was Dylan Thomas, a 'metaphoric' writer if ever there was one.

In the middle of the 1950s, a new generation of writers began to exert an opposite pressure on the pendulum. They were sometimes referred to as 'The Movement' (mainly in the context of poetry) and sometimes, more journalistically, as the 'Angry Young Men' (mainly in the context of fiction and drama). Some of the key figures in these partially overlapping groups were: Kingsley Amis, Philip Larkin, John Wain, D. J. Enright, Thom Gunn, Donald Davie, Alan Sillitoe, John Osborne, Arnold Wesker. Others who shared the same general aims and assumptions as these writers, or contributed to the formation of a distinctively 1950s *écriture*, were William Cooper, C. P. Snow and his wife Pamela Hansford Johnson, Colin McInnes, Angus Wilson, John Braine, Stan Barstow, Thomas Hinde, Keith Waterhouse, David Storey and, in precept if not in practice, Iris Murdoch.[2] The 1950s writers were suspicious of, and often positively hostile to the modernist movement and certainly opposed to any further efforts at 'experimental' writing. Dylan Thomas epitomised everything they detested: verbal obscurity, metaphysical pretentiousness, self-indulgent romanticism, compulsive metaphorising were his alleged faults. They themselves aimed to communicate clearly and honestly their perceptions of the world as it was. They were empiricists, influenced by logical positivism and 'ordinary language' philosophy. The writer of the previous generation they most respected was probably George Orwell.[3] Technically, the novelists were content to use, with only slight modifications, the conventions of 1930s and Edwardian realism. Their originality was largely a matter of tone and attitude and subject matter, reflecting changes in English culture and society brought about by the convulsion of the Second World War – roughly speaking, the supersession of a bourgeois-dominated class-society by a more meritocratic and opportunistic social system. The poets dealt with ordinary prosaic experience in dry, disciplined, slightly depressive verse. In short, they were antimodernist, readerly and realistic, and belong on the metonymic side of our bi-polar scheme.

The most representative writers of this generation were Kingsley Amis and Philip Larkin (significantly they were close friends at Oxford). I have written elsewhere of Amis's work and its relation to modernist writing,[4] so I shall confine myself here to Philip Larkin. That he is an antimodernist scarcely needs demonstration. To find his own poetic voice he had to shake off the influence of Yeats that pervades his first volume of poems, *The North Ship* (1945); and he has made no secret of his distaste for the poetics of T. S. Eliot which underpins so much verse in the modernist tradition. 'I . . . have no belief in "tradition" or a common myth-kitty, or casual allusions in poems to other poems or poets', he has written; and, 'separating the man who suffers from the man who creates is all right – we separate the petrol from the engine – but the dependence of the second on the first is complete.'[5] Like Orwell, Larkin believes that the task of the writer is to communicate as accurately as he can in words experience which is initially non-verbal: poetry is 'born of the tension between what [the poet] non-verbally feels and what can be got over in common word-usage to someone who hasn't had his experience or education or travel-grant.'[6] Like most writers in the antimodernist, or realist or readerly tradition, Larkin is, in aesthetic matters, an antiformalist: 'Form holds little interest for me. Content is everything.'[7]

It would be easy enough to demonstrate abstractly that the last-quoted assertion is an impossibly self-contradictory one for a poet to make. A more interesting line of enquiry, however, is to try and define the kind of form Larkin's work actually has, in spite of his somewhat disingenuous denials. (He has claimed, characteristically, that the omission of the main verb in 'MCMXIV', which so powerfully and poignantly creates the sense of an historical moment, poised between peace and war, arrested and held for an inspection that is solemn with afterknowledge, was an 'accident'[8] – as if there could be such a thing in a good poem.) My suggestion is that we can best accomplish this task of defining the formal character of Larkin's verse by regarding him as a 'metonymic' poet.

Poetry, especially lyric poetry, is an inherently metaphoric mode, and to displace it towards the metonymic pole is (whether Larkin likes it or not) an 'experimental' literary gesture. Such poetry makes its impact by appearing daringly, even shockingly unpoetic, particularly when the accepted poetic mode is elaborately metaphoric. This was true of the early Wordsworth, and it was certainly true of Philip Larkin in his post-*North Ship* verse: nothing could have been more different from the poetry of Dylan Thomas and the other ageing members of the 'New Apocalypse'. Larkin, indeed, has many affinities with Wordsworth (in spite of having had a 'forgotten boredom' of a childhood)[9] and seems to share Wordsworth's 'spontaneous overflow' theory of poetic creation, which T. S. Eliot thought he had disposed of in 'Tradition and the Individual Talent'. 'One should . . . write poetry only when one wants to and has to', Larkin has remarked; and, 'writing isn't an act of will'.[10] His poetic style is characterised by colloquialism, 'low' diction and conscious cliché:

> Coming up England by a different line
> For once, early in the cold new year,
> We stopped, and, watching men with number-plates
> Sprint down the platform to familiar gates,
> 'Why, Coventry!' I exclaimed. 'I was born here.'
>
> > ('I Remember, I Remember')

> > > I lie
> Where Mr Bleaney lay, and stub my fags
> On the same saucer-souvenir, and try
> Stuffing my ears with cotton-wool, to drown
> The jabbering set he egged her on to buy.
> I know his habits – what time he came down,
> His preference for sauce to gravy, why
>
> He kept on plugging at the four aways –
>
> > ('Mr Bleaney')

> When I see a couple of kids
> And guess he's fucking her and she's
> Taking pills or wearing a diaphragm,
> I know this is paradise
>
> Everyone old has dreamed of all their lives –
>
> > ('High Windows')

With Wordsworth, Larkin might claim that his 'principal object . . . was to choose incidents and situations from common life, and to relate or describe them, throughout, as far as was possible in a selection of language really used by men, tracing in them truly, though not ostentatiously, the primary laws of our nature,[11] though it is from common urban-industrial life that he usually chooses them – shops, trains, hospitals, inner-city streets and parks. The gaudy mass-produced glamour of chain store lingerie –

> Lemon, sapphire, moss-green, rose
> Bri-Nylon Baby-Dolls and Shorties

provides the occasion for a tentative, uncondescending meditation
on the mystery of sexual allure:

> How separate and unearthly love is,
> Or women are, or what they do,
> Or in our young unreal wishes
> Seem to be: synthetic, new,
> And natureless in ecstasies.
> ('The Large Cool Store')

The topic of death is handled in contexts where modern urban
folk face it, the ambulance and the hospital:

> All know they are going to die.
> Not yet, perhaps not here, but in the end,
> And somewhere like this. That is what it means,
> This clean-sliced cliff; a struggle to transcend
> The thought of dying, for unless its powers
> Outbuild cathedrals nothing contravenes
> The coming dark, though crowds each evening try
>
> With wasteful, weak, propitiatory flowers.
> ('The Building')

Larkin is a declared realist. 'Lines on a Young Lady's Photograph
Album', strategically placed at the beginning of his first important
collection, *The Less Deceived* (1955), is his 'Musée des Beaux Arts',
taking not Flemish painting but snapshots as the exemplary art
form:

> But o, photography! as no art is,
> Faithful and disappointing! that records
> Dull days as dull, and hold-it smiles as frauds,
> And will not censor blemishes
> Like washing-lines and Hall's-Distemper boards,
>
> But shows the cat as disinclined, and shades
> A chin as doubled when it is, what grace
> Your candour thus confers upon her face!
> How overwhelmingly persuades
> That this is a real girl in a real place,

In every sense empirically true!

Like a realistic novelist, Larkin relies heavily on synecdochic detail to evoke scene, character, culture and subculture. In 'At Grass', the past glories of race horses are evoked thus:

> Silks at the start: against the sky
> Numbers and parasols: outside,
> Squadrons of empty cars, and heat,
> And littered grass: then the long cry
> Hanging unhushed till it subside
> To stop-press columns on the street.

In Hull

> domes and statues, spires and cranes cluster
> Beside grain-scattered streets, barge-crowded water,
> And residents from raw estates, brought down
> The dead straight miles by stealing flat-faced trolleys;
> Push through plate-glass swing doors to their desires –
> Cheap suits, red kitchen-ware, sharp shoes, iced lollies,
> Electric mixers, toasters, washers, driers –
>
> ('Here')

After the Agricultural Show

> The car park has thinned. They're loading jumps on a truck.
> Back now to private addresses, gates and lamps
> In high stone one-street villages, empty at dusk,
> And side roads of small towns (sports finals stuck
> In front doors, allotments reaching down to the railway);
>
> ('Show Saturday')

To call Larkin a metonymic poet does not imply that he uses no metaphors – of course he does. Some of his poems are based on extended analogies – 'Next, Please', 'No Road' and 'Toads', for instance. But such poems become more rare in his later collections. All three just mentioned are in *The Less Deceived*, and 'Toads Revisited' in *The Whitsun Weddings* (1964) makes a fairly perfunctory use of the original metaphor. Many of his poems have no metaphors at all – for example, 'Myxomatosis', 'Poetry of

Departures', 'Days', 'As Bad as a Mile', 'Afternoons'. And in what
are perhaps his finest and most characteristic poems, the
metaphors are foregrounded against a predominantly metonymic
background, which is in turn foregrounded against the background
of the (metaphoric) poetic tradition. 'The Whitsun Weddings' is a
classic example of this technique.

> That Whitsun, I was late getting away:
>   Not till about
> One-twenty on the sunlit Saturday
> Did my three-quarters-empty train pull out,
> All windows down, all cushions hot, all sense
> Of being in a hurry gone. We ran
> Behind the backs of houses, crossed a street
> Of blinding windscreens, smelt the fish-dock; thence
> The river's level drifting breadth began,
> Where sky and Lincolnshire and water meet.

This opening stanza has a characteristically casual, colloquial tone,
and the near-redundant specificity ('One-twenty', 'three-quarters-
empty') of a personal anecdote, a 'true story' (compare
Wordsworth's 'I've measured it from side to side, / 'Tis three feet
long, and two feet wide'). The scenery is evoked by metonymic
and synecdochic detail ('drifting breadth', 'blinding windscreens',
etc.) as are the wedding parties that the poet observes at the
stations on the way to London, seeing off bridal couples on their
honeymoons:

> The fathers with broad belts under their suits
> And seamy foreheads; mothers loud and fat;
> An uncle shouting smut; and then the perms,
> The nylon gloves and jewellery-substitutes,
> The lemons, mauves, and olive-ochres that
>
> Marked off the girls unreally from the rest.

Apart from the unobtrusive 'seamy', there are no metaphors here:
appearance, clothing, behaviour, are observed with the eye of a
novelist or documentary writer and allowed to stand, untrans-
formed by metaphor, as indices of a certain recognisable way of
life. There *is* a simile in this stanza, but it is drawn from the

context (railway stations) in a way that is characteristic of realistic writers using the metonymic mode:

> As if out on the end of an event
>   Waving goodbye
> To something that survived it.

As the poem goes on, Larkin unobtrusively raises the pitch of rhetorical and emotional intensity – and this corresponds to the approach of the train to its destination: the journey provides the poem with its basic structure, a sequence of spatio-temporal contiguities (as in 'Here'). Some bolder figures of speech are introduced – 'a happy funeral', 'a religious wedding'; and in the penultimate stanza a striking simile which still contrives to be 'unpoetic', by collapsing the conventional pastoral distinction between nasty town and nice country:

> I thought of London spread out in the sun,
> Its postal districts packed like squares of wheat.

It is in the last stanza that the poem suddenly, powerfully, 'takes off',[12] transcends the merely empirical, almost sociological observation of its earlier stanzas and affirms the poet's sense of sharing, vicariously, in the onward surge of life as represented by the newly wedded couples collected together in the train ('this frail travelling coincidence') and the unpredictable but fertile possibilities the future holds for them.

> We slowed again,
> And as the tightened brakes took hold, there swelled
> A sense of falling, like an arrow-shower
> Sent out of sight, somewhere becoming rain.

This metaphor, with its mythical, magical and archaic resonances, is powerful partly because it is so different from anything else in the poem (except for 'religious wounding', and that has a tone of humorous overstatement quite absent from the last stanza).

Something similar happens in Larkin's most famous poem, 'Church Going', where the last stanza has a dignity and grandeur of diction:

> A serious house on serious earth it is,
> In whose blent air all our compulsions meet,
> Are recognised, and robed as destinies.

which comes as a thrilling surprise after the downbeat, slightly ironic tone of the preceding stanzas, a tone established in the first stanza:

> Hatless, I take off
> My cycle-clips in awkward reverence.

That line-and-a-half must be the most often quoted fragment of Larkin's poetry, and the way in which the homely 'cycle-clips' damps down the metaphysical overtones of 'reverence' and guarantees the trustworthy ordinariness of the poetic persona is indeed typical of Larkin. But if his poetry were limited to merely avoiding the pitfalls of poetic pretentiousness and insincerity it would not interest us for very long. Again and again he surprises us, especially in the closing lines of his poems, by his ability to transcend – or turn ironically upon – the severe restraints he seems to have placed upon authentic expression of feeling in poetry. Sometimes, as in 'The Whitsun Weddings' and 'Church Going', this is accomplished by allowing a current of metaphorical language to flow into the poem, with the effect of a river bursting through a dam. But quite as often it is done by a subtle complication of metre, line-endings and syntax. For example, the amazing conclusion to 'Mr Bleaney':

> But if he stood and watched the frigid wind
> Tousling the clouds, lay on the fusty bed
> Telling himself that this was home, and grinned,
> And shivered, without shaking off the dread
>
> That how we live measures our own nature,
> And at his age having no more to show
> Than one hired box should make him pretty sure
> He warranted no better, I don't know.

Syntactically this long periodic sentence is in marked contrast to the rest of the poem, and marks a reversal in its drift: a shift from satiric spleen vented upon the external world – a Bleaney-world to which the poetic persona feels superior – to a sudden collapse of his own morale, a chilling awareness that this environment may correspond to his own inner 'nature'. This fear is expressed obliquely by a speculative attribution of the speaker's feelings to Mr Bleaney. The diction is plain and simple (if more dignified than in the preceding stanzas) but the syntax, subordinate clauses burgeoning and negatives accumulating bewilderingly, is extremely complex and creates a sense of helplessness and entrapment. The main clause so long delayed – 'I don't know' – when it finally comes, seems to spread back dismally through the whole poem, through the whole life of the unhappy man who utters it.

Many of Larkin's most characteristic poems end, like 'Mr Bleaney', with a kind of eclipse of meaning, speculation fading out in the face of the void. At the end of 'Essential Beauty', the girl in the cigarette ad becomes a Belle Dame Sans Merci for the 'dying smokers' who

> sense
> Walking towards them through some dappled park
> As if on water that unfocused she
> No match lit up, nor drag ever brought near,
> Who now stands newly clear,
> Smiling, and recognising, and going dark.
>
> We spend all our life on imprecisions,
> That when we start to die
> Have no idea why.
>
> ('Ignorance')

Death is, we can all agree, a 'nonverbal' reality, because, as Wittgenstein said, it is not an experience *in* life; and it is in dealing with death, a topic that haunts him, that Larkin achieves the paradoxical feat of expressing in words something that is beyond words:

> Life is slow dying . . .
> And saying so to some
> Means nothing; others it leaves
> Nothing to be said.
>
> ('Nothing to be Said')

The same theme, I take it, forms the conclusion to the title poem of Larkin's most recent collection, *The High Windows*. The poet compares his generation's envy of the sexual freedom of the young in today's Permissive Society to the putative envy of older people of his own apparent freedom, in his youth, from superstitious religious fears.

> And immediately
> Rather than words comes the thought of high windows:
> The sun-comprehending glass,
> And beyond it, the deep blue air, that shows
> Nothing, and is nowhere, and is endless.

13

Art and Larkin[1]

Barbara Everett

Philip Larkin once dropped the pensive remark (concerning, I think, the reviews of *The Whitsun Weddings*, but it could just have been earlier, in the years after the publication of *The Less Deceived*, when I first got to know him): 'I have no enemies. But my friends don't like me.' It was a joke. But the dislike of the friends of poetry can be interesting, if it is intelligent and honourable. Larkin attracted, all his working life, hostility from a kind of criticism which at its best – either American or more or less based on Cambridge English studies – articulated the opinion that his work was profoundly philistine. I want to praise his writing for precisely this reason: that it made itself permanently vulnerable to such charges. Larkin's poetry helped to continue, I would suggest, a great English or British tradition that has for centuries refused to avail itself of the self-indulgent securities of 'Art', that made itself philistine for the good of the soul of literature.

Larkin and Kingsley Amis share, especially in their earlier work (and I would guess that Larkin initiated it) a practice of 'shocking the bourgeois', but in a special reversed form: needling the aesthetic reader – 'Filthy Mozart' and the rest. Few friends and fewer enemies of Larkin's verse need reminding of these provocations, which also relate back to perfectly serious attitudes. 'A Study of Reading Habits' ('Books are a load of crap') is a self-undermining comic attack on authorial complacency which also defines the circumstances in which the reader, too, may misuse both life and literature simultaneously. All the other gruff jokes involving cycle-clips and Marks nighties and gin-and-tonics, and the even more notorious four-letter words, derive together from the resolution *not* to make the

> deliberate step backwards
> To create an object:
> Books; china; a life

129

Reprehensibly perfect.
('Poetry of Departures')

The most perfectionist aestheticism can, of course, throw off this special contempt for the 'perfect': it is hardly an English philistine who yawns that 'all the rest is *literature*'. But I want to go rather further and try to show that in Larkin's work this feeling for the 'reprehensible' goes deeper, shaping and affecting it at that inexplicit level from which his verse takes so much of its real power. Indeed, a pursuit of truth which is also a flight from 'Art' seems to me to condition the whole development of Larkin's poetry. It is relevant here that Larkin said his ambition was to write novels, works closer to life than poems; indeed, his address from the chair of an earlier Booker Prizegiving is a superb defence of the novel precisely for this truth-to-life.

Larkin's 'development' is itself open to question. Most of the appreciative obituaries published since his death in 1985 have described Larkin as a writer who did not develop. I strongly agree with Alan Brownjohn's original review of *High Windows*, one of the finest Larkin essays we have, that this simply isn't true.[2] There is, in fact, a considerable distance between *The North Ship* and *High Windows*. And I would myself explain the difference in terms of the poet's own conscious struggle to leave behind what he surely saw as the great weakness of the early volume: its helpless artiness. Something in this innocent Yeatsian collection links up with the superficially very different, and better, translation (published by John Fuller's Sycamore Press) which the even younger Larkin, painstakingly following Eliot and other Modernists, took from Baudelaire's 'Femmes Damnées' – the Larkin poem a fascinatingly talented if odd attempt to fuse the 'French' or 'Aesthetic' subject of lesbian passion with a setting in the English philistine green-belt suburbs. And that quality links with the more self-guarding and self-censoring, but still very solemn, two novels that followed *The North Ship*.

The young Larkin took Art very seriously. It was to him more than a profession: it was a calling. The entirely touching and powerful 'Send No Money' from *The Whitsun Weddings* is evidence of this, even without the rest of his career. And very obviously the writer had an amount of talent and intelligence in itself remarkable enough to justify any seriousness. Yet for the Protestant moralist (and Larkin once described himself in conversation as 'one of Nature's Orange-Men') all arts present problems. Even at the technical level, the arty, the merely derivative, the simply pleasing remained the writer's solace and quandary at once. In Larkin's work there is always the temptation towards the perhaps merely pretty which recurs in some of his most popular but weaker poems: 'Church Going', 'An Arundel Tomb', for instance. And an awareness of this weakness for the 'beautiful' seemingly led him to try to compensate in the direction of the 'efficient' (the terms are his own), with results of grossness and hardness including the four-letter words. The two faults that Larkin's poetry comes most triumphantly to avoid are sentimentality, on the one hand, and brutality, on the other.

Larkin's verse develops according to the struggle, perhaps the effort of all true makers, to escape soft personal predilection and allow the poems to commit themselves to lucid strength, to the nature of things as they are beyond the fantasies of the ego. The essential virtue of the last two volumes, and especially of *High Windows*, is the concentration of personal feeling in each poem accompanied by an extreme circumscription of any merely personal expression of the self. Larkin is often described now as a Romantic poet, as he probably is in some sense: but the term explains too little without qualifying questions and explanations. The presence of feeling, and the attribution of feeling to familiar objects doesn't itself constitute Romanticism, unless we are Romantic every time we stroke the cat. What is striking in Larkin's poems is the way in which the simple ceremonies and occasions of feeling (the 'Whitsun weddings') are set forward, in these intensely crafted works of art, to fill the void of the abnegation of poetic authority. Few English Romantic poets have ever said 'I' as little as Larkin; and the pervasive absence of the word is less mere reticence or self-dislike than a strange personal strength, part of the work's haunting power: almost a strategy. 'Here', for instance, which superbly opens *The Whitsun Weddings*, and doesn't contain the word 'I', isn't Hull, but a true private world startlingly voided of egoism: a rich and radiant arrival Northwards at Nowhere. The whole poetic career, in so many ways so prudently managed, is also a drive to extinguish the false artistic ego: it closes with the last true Larkinian poem, 'Aubade', which followed *High Windows* by a few years and took as its subject the writer's own death.

Work that reduces its ego together with its appearance of artifice (the art of what Larkin in a very early poem called

'Modesties') will find an enjoying audience, but at a price. His verse wears an air of artlessness that constitutes its success, but that breeds misconceptions. Not only the very regrettable *Times* obituary but others more sympathetic agreed that the poet was unproductive, his major verse amounting to three slim volumes. This is as questionable as the truism that Larkin never developed. The issue turns on our sense of what poetry is. If we regard Larkin's work as social statements, and the poet as a *'decent chap, a real good sort'*, the old White Major in person – and obituaries are of course bound to pay attention to the decent chap – then the contents of these three volumes could be regarded as the sadly scanty remains of one (though curiously elusive, various and self-contradictory) personality. But as artefacts, created objects, what Larkin calls in 'Show Saturday' 'rows/Of single supreme versions . . . pure excellences that enclose/A recession of skills', these poems are as unpredictably unlike each other as the 'Show' goods themselves. In terms of works of art, Larkin's harvest was quite remarkable: few lyric poets have achieved eighty or ninety poems, all autonomous, all essentially different from each other. And their variety comes, precisely, from that escape from personality which Eliot made us associate with Modernism, but which is an attribute, really, of all disciplined art, especially that of a Puritan-derived or 'philistine' society. The artist as such has no standing, but sets his goods among the 'lambing-sticks, rugs,/Needlework, knitted caps, baskets, all worthy, all well done,/But less than the honeycombs': a bee could do better.

An unobtrusive art, however fine it is, may get itself confused with artlessness – and that, in its turn, with a mere affability. A position shared by several obituaries was that Larkin's work brought poetry back to ordinary people. This is a difficult issue, because people who read poetry are never ordinary people: the habit of reading at all differentiates a person, and the degree of education is largely irrelevant. I once took an adult education class composed of the intelligent under-schooled – a garage mechanic, housewives, an elderly lord of the manor – and the wild success of the course was Beckett's *Endgame*, which was found so funny and so lifelike that the meeting broke up in hysteria. I suspect, in short, that the artistic and under-educated prefer their poetry obscure and elaborate, Metaphysical or Modernist; the Movement was – as it usually is – for tired intellectuals. And, if it is a case of bringing poetry to philistines (a

somewhat different matter) then the success was more Betjeman's
than Larkin's.

Questions of audience are always abstract and difficult. Of
perhaps more interest are what one might call expectations of
response in the work of Larkin and Amis, and in each case these
are complex and ironic. Both work within straightforward social
criteria that involve courtesies and rationalities; but both make use
regularly of means like Larkin's four-letter words which may
offend precisely because they figure in an idiom otherwise so
well-behaved or well-adjusted, even so cautiously temperate.
Whatever there is to say about Larkin's particular poetic medium
is consonant with this. For reasons at once personal, moral and
aesthetic, the poet has found himself, as a painter might do, by
the selection of a restricted palette. In that selection there is a
comparable element of the complex and ironic. Larkin has come
to make his own a field that one might well love especially in
compensation for, or in contradiction to, a lifetime above all shut
up in books, papers, words – the abstract appurtenances of
literary intellect. The poet turns tenderly to the sweet middle
ranges of 'philistine' experience:

> The pictures on
> The walls are comic – hunting, trenches, stuff
> Nobody minds or notices . . .

These lines from 'Livings 1' are by someone who spent his life in
some sense minding and noticing ('The Card-Players', from
elsewhere in *High Windows*, is a remarkable simulacrum of a
seventeenth-century Dutch genre painting). And 'Livings 1' is in
itself a work of art that one could do worse than offer to anyone
who observed, not without point, that our period has produced
little at the level of Eliot, Yeats, Hardy: it is probably as good as
any single short poem written by any of them.

The 'philistinism' of 'Livings 1' is central to the poem, not
incidental; it is 'principled' in a full sense. The lines, spoken in the
first person, define the life of a young commercial traveller who,
inheriting his father's business, in his faithful pursuit of it is
staying the night at a small hotel, somewhere north-easterly or
easterly, in a year that turns out to be 1929 (the first year of the
great economic slump). He dines, he visits the Smoke Room –
where the pictures are comic – and he walks around the square:

> Later, the square is empty: a big sky
> Drains down the estuary like the bed
> Of a gold river, and the Customs House
> Still has its office lit.

The slow, sleepy and cumulative ending of this pellucid poem (with its final *Cavalcade*-like declaration of date) can move a reader to tears. But its power depends neither quite on its magnificent image of an East Anglican evening, lit by half-symbolic meanings, nor on the pathos of the date: but on the slow-building pure factuality of the first two stanzas, and especially the first.

'Livings 1' has an extraordinary sense of place (I once asked Larkin if it were King's Lynn, and the guess was confirmed). But the factuality is something other than *just* a sense of place: it is, rather, a sense of life, and of life. The almost monosyllabic first stanza, describing arrival, dinner, newspaper, begins transparently with the self-introduction of the young businessman: 'I deal with farmers, things like dips and feed'. The much earlier 'Arrivals, Departures' from *The Less Deceived* presents the dawn arriver, the hopeful 'traveller . . . / His bag of samples knocking at his knees'. Amis, too, has an interest in this seediest of social figures, the commercial traveller, and makes his poet the man with 'A Case of Samples'; and in one of the funniest incidents in *Take A Girl Like You*, the schoolmaster-hero tries to impress a formidably beautiful but mean and stupid whore by pretending to be an expense-account businessman, a dealer in such things as dips: 'Goat dip. Horse dip. Pig dip. Donkey dip. Mule dip. Camel dip. Elephant dip . . .'. After a pause for thought: '"How could you dip an elephant?" she asked vigilantly. "An elephant's too big to be dipped."' What we get from the novelist Amis's classics master is a farcical poetic fantasy of the business life ('"You don't actually dip him, you see . . . you more sort of hose him."').[3] It is the Larkin poem – in the first person, and without inverted commas – which takes the commercial traveller *seriously*; the depth of its factuality goes well beyond the novel. Traveller and poet here become one. The 'philistine' conditions, sufficiently loved, offer up an unused, fresh symbol of life in its workaday transience and in its moments, like the poem itself, of fugitive, wasted, inexplicable glory, as the sky shines on the river, and the light is on in the Customs House.

This beautiful and disturbing poem works because it is more

than a conceit; it finds that 'principle' in philistine existence ('things like dips and feed') which makes poet and businessman together 'think it's worth while coming' – a principle that makes a 'living' also a rectitude, as 'the Customs House / Still has its office lit'. In it, Larkin's art goes beyond the clever skills of 'Femmes Damnées' or the fervent feelings (mostly self-absorbed) of *The North Ship*; it has become purely an art of what earlier periods used to call 'invention', a 'finding of the subject', a sense of the real that is also self-knowledge: knowing what the writer is here to write about. 'Things like dips and feed': the phrase itself half-ironically half-salutes that densely actual commonplace existence that all Larkin's poems 'invent' as their subject. In the two 'Toads' poems, one to each of the earlier volumes, there is an element of the sardonic, an unrest in the presentation of the self as mere businessman ('What else can I answer?'). But in 'Livings 1' and sustainedly throughout *High Windows* there is no 'what else'; the condition becomes its own symbol, and is enough, or not enough.

I have stressed this art of 'invention'. The peculiar nature of Larkin's originality may become clearer in the light of an odd fact. I was browsing through a forgotten anthology picked up in some charity sale, and I came across a poem by the late Vivian de Sola Pinto, Professor of English at Nottingham for many years. The anthology was titled *England*, and was put out by the English Association in 1946. The poem is called 'In the Train'; it's a pleasant though unremarkable little poem which would not have caught my attention but for the fact that it evidently caught Larkin's attention very profoundly. The first two of its six stanzas go:

I am in a long train gliding through England,
Gliding past green fields and gentle grey willows,
Past huge dark elms and meadows full of buttercups,
And old farms dreaming among mossy apple trees.

Now we are in a dingy town of small ugly houses
And tin advertisements of cocoa and Sunlight Soap,
Now we are in a dreary station built of coffee-coloured wood
Where barmaids in black stand in empty Refreshment
   Rooms,
And shabby old women sit on benches with suitcases . . .

This artlessly 'philistine' poem furnished Larkin (almost certainly unconsciously) with a surprising quantity of his poetic materials for the rest of his writing career. Pinto's rushing, scrambling account of a train journey north, itself dependent on Auden's 'Night Mail', gave Larkin the phrase 'tin advertisements of cocoa' (see 'MCMXIV); half of another, in 'Afternoon is fading' (see 'Afternoons', which begins 'Summer is fading'); more than one adapted image ('Sunshine flashes on canals and then the rain comes', 'In the murky Midlands where meadows grow more colourless' – see 'The Whitsun Weddings'); and, most of all, the figure of the train journey north as an image of commonplace Romantic experience (see *A Girl in Winter*, 'I Remember, I Remember', 'Here', 'The Whitsun Weddings', 'Dockery and Son').

Yet, as anyone who glances at Pinto's poem realises, none of this matters at all – although it justifies Larkin's generosity in his *Twentieth-Century Verse* to those almost-giftless poets who nourish the great community of writers. Pinto's poem only provided details of 'scenery'; it only suggested a journey. These reservations are required by the distinction between scenery and poetry. In *High Windows* Larkin is a poet 'philistine' and 'businesslike' enough to write a whole poem about, and actually titled, 'Money': a fine and strange poem, not much noticed by critics, one that, uniquely starting from the arrival of a bank-statement ('Quarterly, is it?'), contemplates a lifetime's savings and listens to 'money singing'. But money's song, which tells of all the ordinary riches of life, falls on deaf ears; money becomes 'a provincial town' distantly looked down on from long French windows:

> The slums, the canal, the churches ornate and mad
> In the evening sun. It is intensely sad.

High Windows is a collection which may often still be thought of as celebrating, like the rest of Larkin's work, a real and essentially commonplace England. Certainly the book creates a poetic territory which one could call, if one wants, entirely English, a Kingdom of Philistia. But this is an aesthetic and inward version of middle earth, imagined and rendered with an extraordinary self-consistency and autonomy of tone and texture, subject and ethos; and it is much more original and much odder than it may sound. Its slums, its canal, its churches are 'ornate and mad / In the evening sun'; and it is in more senses than one looked down on from high windows. That creative consciousness in Larkin which made Pinto's poem about England part of the harvest of Philistia, has here mapped out a region that is something other than 'celebrated': a region peculiarly substantial yet, like all material things, full of void, the fabric of a dream. The exquisite seaside poem, 'To the Sea', is full of darknesses, strange vacuities and echoes,

> The distant bathers' weak protesting trebles
> Down at its edge . . .

And in the similarly beautiful 'Cut Grass', the English summer itself is a long breath exhaled, a dying in 'the white hours'.

Larkin's invention of Philistia is best summarised simply by quoting a whole poem. The choice is large, and all are different; but here is one less familiar than some have become, 'Friday Night in the Royal Station Hotel':

> Light spreads darkly downwards from the high
> Clusters of lights over empty chairs
> That face each other, coloured differently.
> Through open doors, the dining-room declares
> A larger loneliness of knives and glass
> And silence laid like carpet. A porter reads
> An unsold evening paper. Hours pass,
> And all the salesmen have gone back to Leeds,
> Leaving full ashtrays in the Conference Room.
>
> In shoeless corridors, the lights burn. How
> Isolated, like a fort,it is –
> The headed paper, made for writing home
> (If home existed) letters of exile: *Now*
> *Night comes on. Waves fold behind villages.*

A sonnet of principled love for Philistia, a one-night hotel at best, the poem ends by seeing its subject as sole bastion of ancient empires but also infinitely fragile, dissolving into that Roman and pre-Roman night. An image of 'home / (If home existed)', the lines are alive with negation and paradox, light that 'spreads darkly', empty chairs that 'face each other' and yet are coloured differently, a dining-room that is 'a larger loneliness', corridors 'shoeless', a paper 'unsold'. This is an England that Pinto's train has hardly travelled to.

Larkin's 'Royal Station Hotel' reaches back to some Dark Age of the imagination, where isolation is a fortress – the isolation, perhaps, of the life of reading and writing. Some small part of its intensity can be glossed in merely literary terms. Not too much should be made of the reading in 'foreign poetry' faithfully carried out by the very young Larkin in pursuit of Art. But I suspect that his verse never lost certain ghostly memories of a larger literary universe, which even helped him (paradoxically) to create his Philistia. The last lines here, with Larkin's quiet transition to a vaster more primal world of exile, always bring to my inner ear a memory of the fact that Eliot's 'East Coker', a poem similarly acquainted with 'Chaos and old Night', evokes dawn with an echo from Eliot's own translation of *Anabase*, St-J. Perse's Symbolist epic of ancient exile and huge nomadic wanderings: 'out at sea the dawn wind/Wrinkles and slides'. Something comparable happens at the end of the last fully characteristic poem Larkin wrote, 'Aubade'. This starts philistinely enough with 'I work all day, and get half drunk at night', moves through its confrontation of death, then ends wonderfully with its evocation of a new dawn. Somewhere within its rising rhythm at the end there stirs a memory of a famous poem that Larkin probably read when young, 'Le Cimetière Marin' by Valéry – with the unforgettable last stanza that begins: *Le vent se lève . . . il faut tenter de vivre.* Some ironical ghost of that phrase moves within Larkin's 'Aubade', as is hinted perhaps by its French title. An aubade was an ancient dawn-song of love; Larkin finishes with a grim yet loving evocation of the working world come back in its reality again, the world of 'locked-up offices' with the phones getting ready to ring, and all the 'uncaring/Intricate rented world' beginning to rouse:

> The sky is white as clay, with no sun.
> Work has to be done.
> Postmen like doctors go from house to house.

The very great power of this ending has nothing to do with any French – or any other English – poet, though Larkin's peculiar stoical modesty perhaps gains depth from comparisons with other traditions. 'Work has to be done' is a line that would surely weaken in any other language than English, but in English has a quite classic strength. And the final postman ('like doctors') are purely Larkinian. Poems perhaps are 'letters of exile' too, carried by poet-postmen every day 'from house to house'. The true density of this image shows how serious the 'philistine' art could be. In this sense, Larkin's work not only 'had to be done', but was done.

14

Larkin's Humanity Viewed from Abroad

Bruce K. Martin

In his tribute to Philip Larkin written soon after the poet's death, John Wain, Larkin's friend since their Oxford days, began by observing that Larkin probably would never be a favourite with American readers, partly because their unfamiliarity with things British would likely lead to faulty readings, and because American poetry and poetics, especially in this century, had hardly prepared them to appreciate the precision and accuracy of Larkin's writing. 'The last considerable American poet to have vital links with English poetry was Robert Frost', Wain noted, taking for granted that at this late date no Britisher could manage to re-establish such links.[1] Later in the same essay Wain further observed that the human content of Larkin's poetry is so obvious as hardly to need discussion.

It seems to me, though, that it is precisely Larkin's humanity which most needs discussion in assessing his impact in America. It is that dimension of his writing which allows the Larkin poem to touch the American reader and thus transcend the difficulties posed either by allusions to British institutions and customs or by what Wain termed the 'contained quality' of Larkin's verse. Surely I am not alone in having seen American students, of university age and even younger, taking not only to the standard Larkin 'hits' found in anthologies but to such relatively uncelebrated poems as 'Dry-Point', 'Essential Beauty' and 'To the Sea'. For many such readers – and nowadays the concept of 'university student' reaches well into middle age and beyond – there is immediate recognition of a true poet, one who realises not only the Wordsworthian ideal of a man speaking to men but, ironically, even Whitman's aim of bridging gaps of age, nationality and social class. For all of his professed insularity, Larkin has managed, as have almost none of his fellow Englishmen writing poetry after

140

the First World War, to move and amuse a wide range of American readers.

Because Larkin's writing is accessible, he puts at ease readers likely to distrust not only British poetry (assumed by many to be stuffy, formal and remote) but, indeed, all poetry. This latter, and greater, distrust has been spawned by the very sort of 'difficulty' principle and its accompanying academic apparatus so disparaged by Larkin in his essays and in the example of his own poems. Perhaps even more than in Britain, the modernist revolution in English-language poetry, the central figures of which were almost exclusively American, produced among many academics in the United States a disdain for clarity and common sense and an approval of obscurity as a prime poetic principle. This may have been a peculiarly American attempt to disprove the charge of provincialism levelled by Pound and Eliot by 'out-moderning' the moderns. This is not to say that such an effort was universal in the United States or to discredit the great modern poets themselves – the fault lay almost exclusively with their worshippers – but simply to observe that the tone and practice of many critics and teachers for decades scared off readers not only from modern poetry but from all poetry, which they assumed to be approachable only through esoteric interpretive practices or a slavish dependence on critical commentary.

In his way, then, Philip Larkin, like Frost before him, helped take the wraps off the mystique of poetry, in the United States as well as in England, and there is every reason to believe he will continue to do so. While we Americans often underestimate or overestimate the significance of what our English counterparts recognise readily as everyday references in Larkin's poetry – and sometimes fail to catch their significance altogether – the result is rarely absolute misreading. American readers respond to the emotional range, the wit and the perceptiveness of Larkin's writing, all of which emerge through his contained style. With relief they notice that his poetry is not markedly 'modern' – whatever its affinities to French symbolism and other modernist practices which Larkin's critics have been finding lately[2] – and, as a corollary, that his technique rarely calls attention to itself. Rather than technically complex, his poems appear emotionally complex. But, because their technical virtuosity is understated, Larkin's poems often cause readers to ask, 'How does he do it?' and thus engage in the sort of technical analysis the poems seem designed to prevent. Admiration for the poetry thus runs full circle, though its base continues to be the humanity always evident in Larkin's writing.

One way in which this humanity manifests itself is suggested by an unlikely source. In section nine of *The Poetics*, Aristotle observes that 'poetry is a more philosophical and higher thing than history: for poetry tends to express the universal, history the particular'.[3] He goes on to explain that while the historian is tied to 'what has happened', the poet is free – indeed, obligated by the nature of what he is about – to deal with 'what may happen'. Even when treating a historical subject the poet must go beyond the facts available to him by inventing and filling in characteristics and actions in accord with the peculiar plan of the 'poem' he is constructing. For Aristotle this could include drama, and for modern readers, works of prose fiction. Therefore, whenever the historian moves out of 'what has happened' to do some filling in of his own, he presumably begins to behave as a poet, and the history he thus constructs begins to take on the formal qualities of a well-made poem or novel. Of course, by suggesting that poetry is more philosophical than history by virtue of its being more universal, Aristotle implies that philosophy is the most universal of the three. Because the philosopher by definition deals with universals, whenever he invents hypothetical examples he must appropriate such poetic skills as plotting and characterisation to make his illustrations effective.

The poet, therefore, enjoys a freedom foreign to the historian or the philosopher's most characteristic practice. Indeed, Aristotle's brief remarks may carry even greater force for literature in the modern world. Because the poet can fill in speculatively, he can delve into the human mind and human behaviour – he can enlarge our sense of ourselves – as can neither the psychiatrist nor the psychologist, bound as they are to particular cases and experiments. The godlike authority and creativity traditionally ascribed to the author become vivid when compared with the entrapment suffered not only by the historian or social scientist, but by the scientist as well. Of course, poetry's advantage over philosophy continues, as the universality of literature arises out of the motives, behaviour and situations of specific persons brought into existence by the poet, playwright or novelist.

The point here is that more than most other recent poets writing in English, Philip Larkin has satisfied the requirements of literature's peculiarly humanist calling. Certainly one need not look far for 'philosophical' concerns in his writing. The preoccupation with time running throughout his work connects Larkin with the mainstream of western philosophy, from the ancient Greeks to the present. This sense of the mystery of time – Larkin's asking what it means and what it doesn't mean – informs much of his mature writing: from such pieces as 'Next, Please', 'I Remember, I Remember' and 'Whatever Happened?' out of the 1950s; through various *Whitsun Wedding* poems ('Dockery and Son', 'Send No Money', 'Reference Back', 'As Bad as a Mile', and 'Days'); and into selections from *High Windows*, notably the title poem, 'Forget What Did' and 'Money'. Perhaps his most concentrated encounter with this issue comes in an early poem, 'Triple Time', where he speaks of the present ('This empty street') as 'A time unrecommended by event', and yet notes, with a mixture of wonder and sadness, how the present was the future anticipated in childhood as 'an air lambent with adult enterprise' and will eventually become the past regretted for unseized opportunity ('A valley cropped by fat neglected changes').

For Larkin the puzzle of time and ephemerality seems especially dramatised by human love and sexuality. The people of his poetry – the speakers and the observed characters, the married and the unmarried – never get it quite right, partly because there seems to be not enough time. Botched opportunity gives way too quickly to the sense that opportunity is gone for good. And, almost always when dealing with the imperfection of our time-filled lives, Larkin invokes semi-Platonic imagery to suggest the desired state of affairs which life fails to deliver. Thus 'Dry-Point', written several years even before *The Less Deceived* appeared, set a mode continuing through his last poems. Like Donne and Keats, Larkin here ties sexuality to time – first by wittily labelling it a 'time-honoured irritant' and then by describing the process of desire and momentary satisfaction immediately giving way to post-coital depression. Here, as in other poems, he finds the pursuer of sexual pleasure deceived into thinking satisfaction would be lasting when, in fact, it led to an even more painful recognition of our distance from 'that padlocked cube of light' toward which we reach in all our significant gestures. In this instance, though, Larkin includes the embittering knowledge that desire, represented by the sex drive, is not to be controlled or denied; the only escape from its irritation is death, hardly an attractive alternative. By the poem's end the most desirable state, and thus the most impossible, has become a place not where desire is satisfied, but where it is not entertained. The 'bare and sunscrubbed' room, filled with Platonic light, takes on a wholly negative cast, scarcely distinguishable from darkness.

Certainly the historical element of Larkin's writing is as pervasive as the philosophical, and perhaps more noticeable to American readers. Taken together, his poems afford a remarkable panorama of British life at mid-century, particularly as it has been lived in the towns of the North and Midlands. In one of his most sustained efforts in this regard, 'Here' (the opening poem to *The Whitsun Weddings*), Larkin captures with loving detail the natural and human landscapes in and around Hull, where he spent the second half of his life. In four stanzas he approaches the 'surprise of a large town' – where 'domes and statues, spires and cranes cluster / Beside grain-scattered streets'; notes, as in several other poems, the staples of retail trade – such things as 'red kitchenware, sharp shoes, iced lollies, / Electric mixers, toasters, washers, driers'; and finally turns his attention to the people (a 'cut-priced crowd', he terms them, 'urban yet simple'), before characteristically reflecting on their 'removed lives'. Elsewhere he devotes entire poems to such various aspects of common life as billboards ('Essential Beauty'), religious evangelism ('Faith Healing'), graffiti ('Sunny Prestatyn') and the workingman's department store ('The Large Cool Store').

Such poems show that Larkin could behave as both a philosopher and a historian. But, even his most blatantly 'philosophical' or 'historical' writing is at least accompanied by the first-person pronoun, singular or plural, to effect some sense of a concrete fictive personality. More typical than what we find in 'Dry-Point' or 'Triple Time', though, is the introduction of people besides the speaker, usually of some degree of specified personality themselves. It is in the subsuming of philosophical and historical elements to more strictly literary demands, and the manner in which Larkin and his speakers respond to the people around them, that he shows us how a true poet behaves. However fashionable it has become to insist that his first collection, *The North Ship*, is not nearly so weak as he or critics believed and to find links between it and *High Windows*, it seems significant that the poems for which he first gained recognition – and for which, it appears likely, he will continue to be recognised – are those which followed upon the writing of two novels and many years of trying to write a third. Larkin himself referred to his novels as 'oversized poems' in their preciseness of detail and language.[4] It seems equally valid to think of his mature poems as miniature novels in terms of the concretely fictional quality they exude. And it is through this quality that his poetizing, the distinctive humanity of his writing, becomes most evident.

As a true poet, Larkin persistently speculates on the lives and fates of those he observes. Observation, which consists of trying to fill in the gaps and indeterminacies created by what he sees directly, thus becomes no casual or passive matter. The poem 'Afternoons' is coloured by the quiet intensity with which he watches young mothers at the playground and imagines, in brief but poignant detail, their husbands and homes and the way in which 'Something is pushing them/To the side of their own lives'. The problem of understanding what is observed or experienced and the concentration required of such an operation are suggested in 'Whatever Happened?', where Larkin, characteristically preoccupied with time's passing, uses the metaphor of photography for the vivid but misleading sensations of memory. Time seems necessary for perspective, but time makes the past moment 'kodak-distant'. Knowledge consists of two kinds of knowing, the immediate and the reflective, which life unfortunately does not permit us simultaneously. Hence the human impulse to fill in for one or the other – 'scene' or 'summary', to use Henry James's distinction. Hence the poet in each of us, Larkin seems to say.

Sometimes he makes the photography metaphor almost literal, as we see him working with actual photos and trying to uncover, or recover, the truth behind them. The swain in 'Lines on a Young Lady's Photograph Album' eagerly searches snapshots as a way of possessing his girlfriend, only to realise the futility of that gesture and the small compensation for losing her which any photos can provide. More elaborately and more successfully, in 'MCMXIV' Larkin moves behind a photograph of First World War vintage to create a whole epoch about to disappear as the war develops: from the lines of urban recruits, he moves through the details of coins, children's names and advertisements into the countryside and the huge estates, to wonder at the 'innocence' which from his dual perspective has both passed and is about to pass. Like Homer in Aristotle's vision of the poet transcending history,[5] Larkin takes the historical artefact and in a few stanzas makes from it something compelling.

In other poems other kinds of artefacts work just as well to inspire the poetic activity. Both 'Faith Healing' and 'At Grass' were the results of Larkin's watching newsreels – of an American evangelist at work and of retired racehorses respectively. In the first he takes us incredibly close to the main action, invoking physical and emotional details far beyond what he could see directly. His imagination alone affords us the feelings of the women blessed by the healer ('as if a kind of dumb / And idiot child within them still survives / To re-awake at kindness') and allows him to see them as emblematic of the regret most people feel at not having been more loved. 'At Grass', composed in the 1940s during Larkin's transition from novelist to poet, not only goes back into the racehorses' careers, to evoke their championships and fame, but speculates on their feelings at present. This seems a perfectly plausible manoeuvre, but taken out of the poem it is absurd. 'Do memories plague their ears like flies?' he asks, only to return to the film by answering, 'They shake their heads'. Concluding that 'they / Have slipped their names', he ascribes 'what must be joy' to creatures who, unlike us, can forget their youth and glory and thus romp unregretfully. Again the pressing issues of time and memory for Larkin, and again the humanist speculation about other – in this instance radically other – ways of coping with them.

Of course, sometimes reading can as easily inspire such speculation as can seeing something pictorial. The poem 'Deceptions' constitutes ample evidence of the power of the printed word – here a single sentence from Mayhew's *London Labour and London Poor* – to jump off the page and set the poet to his work. Usually for Larkin, though, it is the visual which provokes his most intense poeticising. Thus 'Essential Beauty' finds him, in Lewis Carroll fashion, adding a third dimension to the flat, beckoning images of billboard advertising. Relatedly but more subtly, in 'Sunny Prestatyn' he interprets obscene decorations on a travel poster as a gesture toward realism and an understandable expression of contempt for the poster's illusory attractions. Titch Thomas, the graffiti artist unknown but for his name, thus receives from the poet not only a motive but, indeed, a philosophical posture to account for his destructive urges. In finding the graphic or pictorial record more often relevant as a stimulus for poetry, Larkin implicitly confesses his sense of the commonplace and physically concrete as the elements in which we all, whatever our intellectual pretensions, conduct our lives. Even a poem inspired by that most abstract of arts, music, fastens on the single concrete sound – 'That note you hold, narrowing and rising' ('For Sidney Bechet') – as the base upon which to construct an imaginary New Orleans.

All of this is in keeping with the tug of fictionality persisting throughout Larkin's career. Indeed, the poems most celebrated in each of his mature collections fasten primarily on what I have termed the 'poetic' activity of speculatively filling in gaps. In many of his most moving poems Larkin displays his poet-self as a humane model for coping with the puzzles and trials of life. 'Church Going' – the pivotal stanzas of which show him trying to flesh out the abstract 'very last [person] to seek/This place for what it was' – turns on a kind of futuristic speculation, extending infinitely ('someone will forever be surprising/A hunger in himself'). Similarly, the new occupant of Mr Bleaney's room feels compelled to 'see' imaginatively his deceased predecessor, and implicitly to scrutinise the motives behind the caustic tone of his vision, before he can own up to the limitations of his insight into Bleaney or, for that matter, anyone else.

Perhaps the most dramatic instance of poetic filling in as central activity, though, comes in 'High Windows', the first two-thirds of which consists solely of speculation. Indeed, the opening sentence points to the middle-aged speaker's habitual reliance on such activity: 'When I see . . ./And guess . . ./I know this is paradise'. Literally seeing 'a couple of kids' together causes him, almost reflexively, to 'guess' at the casualness of their sexual relations and thus to 'know' all about them he feels he needs to know. But then, he admits to engaging next in a more refined version of the same process, by which he speculatively frames an earlier spectator: 'I wonder if/Anyone looked at me, forty years back,/And thought *That'll be the life*'. Only by such speculation, such imagining, can he gain perspective on what he is doing now when he 'sees' the young people. Only by such speculation can he draw the analogy between his presuming to know them and the presumptuous guesswork of the speculator 'forty years back' regarding his own emancipation from religion. Wondering about others in the present thus leads to wondering about others wondering in the past, and ultimately to a realisation of his error, a corrective view of the 'couple of kids' and an implicit but intense empathy with them. Just as freedom from religious bonds has only compounded the quandary of knowing metaphysically, so, he realises, the sexual revolution has, if anything, only confused the issues of love and sexuality for its supposed beneficiaries. Essentially they have been freed no more than was he. Indeed, the entire poem suggests that the only freedom unconditionally available to the speaker, to the 'couple of kids', and to us – the only freedom in which we can truly revel — is the freedom of the mind to guess, to speculate and to imagine; in other words, the freedom to behave as a poet.

Other poems show the same process at work: 'The Whitsun Weddings', where the unmarried narrator imagines wedding receptions and the married lives just beginning; 'An Arundel Tomb', where Larkin imagines what the entombed earl and countess could not have thought, thus implying what they could; and many more. The Larkin poem typically encourages the reader to be a poet, at least in the sense of noticing, wondering and speculating. At the same time, it reminds us that speculation is never-ending. Larkin's critics, myself included, have probably tended to overplay the degree of closure in his poems. Though, to be sure, they all do end in a literal sense, they often conclude by raising as many questions as they have resolved. It is fine for Larkin's church-goer to have recognised the impulse behind his church-going, but doesn't the poem's ending replace one uncertainty with another by asking in what frame of mind, other than even greater self-consciousness, he can again enter a church? Might consciousness of his motive make him, ironically, less motivated in the future? To ask such questions is not to violate the spirit of the poem, for Larkin has very clearly located the poem's ultimate outcome far beyond the printed page, in an indefinite future. Likewise, while the suddenly humbled tenant in 'Mr Bleaney' may now recognise the deathlike trap in which he is living, without even the consolations of family and friends enjoyed by Bleaney, does such recognition signal the beginning of greater humaneness or a first step toward suicidal despair? The poem asks us to speculate on precisely what sort of progress has been made: toward life or toward death, hope or regret, society or isolation. And, these same dualities inform the tonal tensions in most of Larkin's other writings, as well.

Even the rehearsal in 'High Windows' of the speaker's habitual way of closing the gap between himself and 'kids' provokes some question as to why he habitually forgets and why he has needed to rely so repeatedly on the sort of symbolic gimmick shown in the final stanza: 'Rather than words comes the thought of high windows'. For all of the warmth evoked by this conclusion, does it not create some doubt as to the speaker's sincerity or at least suggest his evasion of the real moral issue at the heart of both his forgetting and his remembering? Again, to ask such questions is not to deconstruct the poem beyond the terms intended by Larkin himself, in whose poetry uncertainty resonates at least as strongly as conviction, but to suggest how his endings often represent non-endings by inviting, indeed demanding, a measure of scepticism. This very scepticism constitutes speculation's reverse side, that force which keeps the poet correcting his speculations by finding new indeterminacies and writing new poems.

The conflicting urges to know and to doubt colour all of Larkin's poetry with an honesty apparent and endearing to thoughtful readers in America and Britain alike. Both his ongoing search for certainty and his continual confession of uncertainty link him with Hardy as a master of melancholy scepticism. Larkin's pre-eminence among British poets of his generation and his following across the Atlantic confirm the advantage ascribed to poets by Aristotle – an advantage available to us all in our humanness but too often overlooked or undervalued. Larkin's poems quietly but emphatically celebrate that advantage and commend it to us. His success confirms, too, the power of humanist endeavour to persist in an age often wanting in humanism. 'What will survive of us is love', he asserts at the end of 'An Arundel Tomb'. What will survive of Philip Larkin's poetry, on both sides of the Atlantic, is its loving humanity.

Part Three
In Retrospect

15

A Personal Memoir

Hilary Kilmarnock

I

I first met Philip Larkin about 1946. He used to come up for weekends to Oxford to see his friends: having done all his degrees while they were in the army, and so on, he was the only one with a proper job at the time. His friends were mostly St John's undergraduates or former schoolfriends from Coventry, such as Graham Parkes, 'Miud' Richards, Christopher Tosswill and Kingsley Amis. These were the ones he saw most and we used to go around a lot together. It was always a highlight when Philip arrived for a few days. We would usually eat in the British Restaurant, go to each other's digs or college rooms, play jazz records and go to pubs. I was so besotted by Kingsley that it was hard for me to take too much notice of anyone else, but as things calmed down a bit after Kingsley and I were married, we all became very good friends.

Philip was always wonderfully, gloomily witty. His jokes were usually self-deprecating, involving early thinning of hair, stuttering and how horrible life was in general. He was also very funny about the lack of beautiful schoolgirls clamouring for his attention and about what he and Kingsley used to call priest-bait. During the often quite lengthy intervals between visits, Kingsley and Philip had a very good correspondence going: it was always a red-letter day when the postman delivered a letter from Philip, and Kingsley would answer it almost at once.

When he came to stay with us, after Kingsley and I had rented a cottage in Eynsham and started a family, he was always very tidy and used to put our shoes in very neat rows; he also took a lot of photographs – mainly family groups, me holding the first born, and so forth. Later, when we moved to our first house in Swansea, he would write very nice letters to me, always ending them with an illustration of the same little creature wearing a sort of cloak, doing things like hanging up nappies or pushing prams. On the birth of our daughter he sent a poem called 'Born Yesterday'. I was thrilled and touched. One morning when he was staying with us – he had arrived after the children had been put to bed – he had got up in his dressing-gown and was surveying our very steep and weedy small garden. Our eldest son, then about four, came rushing back into the kitchen saying: 'What is it? I don't like it.' I suspect Philip had made a nasty face at him. He always used to tip the boys at the end of his visit, say sixpence for the eldest who is his godson, and threepence for the younger one. These were always compared with the extravagant tips that the younger one's godfather, Bruce Montgomery, used to give them on his visits. Philip liked our various cats and kittens but feared greatly for their safety, being sure that any child around would torture them.

Bruce Montgomery, Kingsley and later George Gale would have jocular chats about who would be the most famous and earn the most money, become lords and such like, but I do not remember Philip ever discussing this.

After Kingsley and I were divorced I lost touch with Philip, but wrote to him once from Spain, where I had been living for some years. He replied very promptly, saying how amazed he was that I actually liked Filthy Abroad. A Harvard student who was visiting, borrowed the letter forthwith – he was doing a thesis on Philip – and didn't return it. A lot of my photographs of Philip have gone that way too, but I still have one when he had a really good thatch of hair, taken while he was up at Oxford.

Sometimes in Spain I would get English and American friends to come down to the rough campo house where we lived. After tapas and vino we would play old records of Benny Goodman, Sidney Bechet and Louis Armstrong and a few other surviving oldies and, on what turned out to be one of the best nostalgia evenings I can remember, I also played my one remaining record of Philip reading some of his own poems, on a small torch battery record player (we had no electricity). I always played the records in one of the downstairs rooms: they were all in such bad condition from so much moving around, being left out in the sun and so on, but with the shutters and doors left open for sound, the effect was pretty good. On this occasion it was quite an experience in the lush moonlit patio, with all the vino tinto being swigged down, hearing Philip's dour dry English voice come over. I think he reads his own poetry better than any other poet I've heard. One of our guests remarked: 'Fancy coming all this way to hear the Master in person.'

I've always had a great respect for Philip and I hope he goes on writing for many years to come.

II

Sadly, it was only four short years after I wrote my personal memoir of Philip that he died on 2 December 1985 at the age of 63.

His illness had lasted six months. After his operation he went home to the house in Hull he now shared with Monica Jones. She was herself suffering from very painful shingles, so one can well imagine how difficult it was for them and how depressing. He would ring up occasionally, or Kingsley and I would ring him up for a short chat, and he and Kingsley wrote to each other during this period. Philip's last letter, which was dated 21 November 1985, was dictated to his secretary because he was no longer able to write. In it he was very funny and rude about Dylan Thomas's collected letters, which had just been published. He wrote affectionately about our daughter Sally, who had sent him her photograph which had arrived just that morning. He knew he was very ill, but perhaps not that he had such a short time left. 'I simply cannot imagine resuming normal life again, whatever that is', he wrote, and he ended by saying, 'I really feel this year has been more than I deserve; I suppose it's all come at once, instead of being spread out as with most people.'

A few days before he died I 'phoned and Monica answered, saying he didn't feel up to talking, so I just sent my love. The next evening the phone rang and it was Philip sounding very weak. I asked him how he felt and he said he felt dreadful and kept losing his balance – pills as well as drink, he said. I remembered another occasion when I asked him what was his tipple, he had told me he found a glass of port very comforting first thing. He didn't keep it by his bed but left it in the dining-room on purpose; it was the only thing that got him up, he said. But nowadays, he told me, he just drank cheap red wine; he couldn't take anything else, nor beer or spirits any longer. I tried to cheer him up and told him to lash out on some expensive wine. When Kingsley heard about the conversation he ordered a case of very good wine to be sent to him at once, but within the next day or two he had died.

I had written to Philip some time back, after he was first taken ill, to suggest a visit – just to pop in – no meal or any trouble to be taken on our account, but he had written back explaining in his usual well-mannered way that it would all be too much for him.

Kingsley, Charles Monteith, Andrew Motion and his wife and I travelled up by train to Hull for Philip's funeral on 9 December 1985. It was a misty, damp, cold day. We were met by Mr Terry Wheldon, his solicitor, who gave us a nice lunch in his home. Monica, on her doctor's advice, did not attend the service, nor was anyone asked to go back to Philip's house. We were sorry about this as we had never seen the place he had lived in for so many years, but it was definite that no one was to go there – Monica was ill herself and must have been dreadfully exhausted after the whole ordeal of being with Philip when he felt so rotten. His sister and niece, his only close relatives, were at the funeral.

The church, St Mary the Virgin in the village of Cottingham, was packed with University and local people. Kingsley gave the address and the service was moving and to the point. Philip had been a non-believer, almost against his desire to be one – anything to make perhaps more bearable the dread of death he always had. He was pulled towards churches, as his poems s⊦ ˙w. After we had been to the graveside with just a few otl. peuple, Mr Wheldon took us back to his h ɔuse for tea. We went out into the garden and could see the tops of the towers of the Hull bridge showing above the mist. Philip had written about it in his poem, 'Bridge for the Living', which he wrote to be set to music and sung at the opening ceremony in Hull in 1981. It was a gloomy and sad train ride back to London.

The Memorial Service on 14 February 1986 in Westminster Abbey was again packed. It was made even sadder, but aroused great feeling, with the reading of 'Church Going' and 'An Arundel Tomb' and the playing of Sidney Bechet's slow blues, 'Blue Horizon', and 'Davenport Blues' (Bix Beiderbecke) by a band organised by Michael Bowen of Hull. The jazz was properly played and Philip would have approved.

Then last October (1986) Kingsley and I went to an exhibition of Philip's life and work held in the library of University College, London, after it had been shown in Hull. This seemed very final and slightly eerie. On glass-topped tables there were manuscripts and typescripts, a work book, unpublished poems, letters, including ones he wrote as Librarian, badges of the honours he received, and photographs of him dated from 1941, library staff groups, jazz players he admired and two of Guy the famous gorilla at London Zoo. Finally, we watched a moving and impressive video of Philip talking about his poems with John Betjeman, who read some of them. There were views of parks and streets in Hull and the country round it, with Philip on his bike visiting churchyards and churches. The video showed me how close his poetry was to the life he saw around him.

I was left with a sense of loss and a feeling I'd been privileged to have known him for such a long time. He always put a brave and charming face on things, even if he felt, and sometimes wrote, to the contrary.

16

Philip Larkin's Inner World

John Bayley

Philip Larkin's death at the age of sixty-three not only means a sad day for English poetry but echoes the deaths of poets in a more romantic era – Shelley drowned, Keats dying of consumption. Larkin was not a young poet cut short in the fullness of his creative life – far from it – and yet something of their legend hangs about him. Like Housman he was a Romantic born out of his age; and it is ironic that his poetry was none the less identified, not long since, as wholly in keeping with the drab, diminished, unillusioned spirit of post-war Britain, a poetry of low-keyed vernacular honesty, whose every line seemed to be saying: 'Come off it'.

It must have given Larkin some wry amusement to have been hailed at that time as 'the laureate of the housing estates'. He was an expert showman, and he knew it, and like all showmen he knew how to seem wholly in touch with his public. He was also a connoisseur of classical jazz, and this gives a clue to the sense in which he lived in the past. In England many people do, and of Larkin's poetry it could be said – as he himself wrote in an introduction to the American edition of John Betjeman's poets – it 'could only happen in England'.[1] For the greater irony is that in England his poetry had the popularity associated with other kinds of late Romanticism – Housman's Shropshire Lad and Barrie's Peter Pan and Betjeman's Joan Hunter Dunn. Like theirs, Larkin's poetic image sold in thousands, achieved a kind of plangent-comic national status.

Yet he was a very private man, and his private world was quite another one. If he touched the national nerve and appealed to the common reader, it was because he could be felt to be leading a double life – again as most people do. Behind the unsentimental directness and the refusal to play the part of poet or intellectual there was a quietly erudite and intensive inner life, a reticent romanticism. Larkin makes the 'one life one writing' formula of a

Lowell or a Berryman seem all surface exposure, a too coherent and explicable unity. Though he seemed so direct Larkin hated to explain. And he had nothing in common with the poets who write for academics and for other poets, the university-funded tribes of Ben with their handouts from government culture and their eagerness to explain on the radio and television what their poetry is trying to do.

A possible key to Larkin's inner world is that he did not want to be a poet so much as a novelist. While still at Oxford in wartime he wrote a novel called *Jill*, which is about a young man at Oxford. For comfort and protection against the dauntingly upper-class life around him he invents a fantasy girl called Jill, whose style and attraction he describes to his friends. Then he sees the actual Jill of his imagination riding past him on a bicycle. He gets to know her, with sad and comical results. Slight as it is the novel is saturated in the Larkinian style of poetry, although at the time that poetry hardly existed and he had found no voice of his own. Later poems were to evoke a Jill-like figure, wearing a bathing suit in 'Sunny Prestatyn', an image defaced on a billboard ('She was too good for this life'), or the model girl of a cigarette brand – 'that unfocused she / No match lit up, nor drag ever brought near' – who visits the dying smoker

> newly clear,
> Smiling, and recognising, and going dark.
> ('Essential Beauty')

An ironic image, in view of the lung and throat cancer that killed Larkin.

Jill was followed by *A Girl in Winter*, which is a real masterpiece, a quietly gripping novel, dense with the humour that is Larkin's trademark, and also an extended prose poem. The author was still only twenty-one. Neither novel made any stir at the time and Larkin wrote no more novels, though he began and abandoned several. Like Keats he had written his *Lamia* and his *Eve of St Agnes* (which the two stories curiously resemble: Larkin read the English course at Oxford), and creative impulse in that direction seems to have dried up. The novelist Kingsley Amis, who was at the same Oxford college and had been a close friend since their undergraduate days, suggested that Larkin was too diffident and conscious of possible failure to thrive in the cut and thrust of the novelists' world. His marvellous sense of things and people ('Mr Bleaney', 'Dockery and Son') became the luminous mirror for a poem rather than being pursued in a more extrovert way through the events of an extended history. However that may be, a poet was born to succeed the aborted novelist.

Gestation was still slow, although a first collection, *The North Ship*, contained some hints of what was to come. Over the years Larkin was working as a librarian, successively at the Universities of Leicester, Belfast and Hull, and short books appeared at ten-year intervals – *The Less Deceived* (1955), *The Whitsun Weddings* (1964), *High Windows* (1974). Though he unforgettably imaged regular work as a toad ('Why should I let the toad *work* / Squat on my life?') he performed it faithfully and with his own kind of drive, needing it as Wallace Stevens needed his insurance office, and ruefully admitting as much in 'Toads Revisited'.

> Give me your arm, old toad;
> Help me down Cemetery Road.

The toad could turn into Larkin's muse, was perhaps the same creature in disguise, and the idea of such visitation – like the moon goddess visiting Endymion – was unexpectedly appropriate for his poetry. In spite of its memorableness and popularity there is always something mysterious about it, and when in the last years of his life Larkin virtually ceased to write poetry he remarked: 'I didn't abandon poetry. Poetry abandoned me.'[2]

With a sensibility as individual and as original as Betjeman's, he and his poems none the less hugged a persona of depression, sterility, absence. 'Deprivation is for me', he once observed, 'what daffodils were for Wordsworth.' A sardonic enemy of the Good Life, he never took holidays abroad, never visited America, spoke of 'foreign poetry' as something quite outside his taste and experience. Yet his book of essays and reviews, *Required Writing*, reveals wide sympathies, deep and trenchant perceptions, a subterranean grasp of the whole of European culture. And indeed the cult of 'deprivation' in his verse has as much animation and relish in it as has Baudelaire's cult of spleen: the authentic and in both cases wholly personal note of Romanticism finding the fattest reward for poetry in its own sense of the unfitness of things.

One of Larkin's last, uncollected, poems ('Aubade') begins, 'I work all day and get half drunk at night', and goes on to descant with an almost joyful eloquence on the fear of death and the terror of extinction. The fear is all too genuine but the fact of the poetry overcomes it – a very traditional feat – as it overcomes the emptiness it evokes so majestically at the end of 'Dockery and Son'.

> Life is first boredom, then fear.
> Whether or not we use it, it goes,
> And leaves what something hidden
>   from us chose,
> And age, and then the only end of age.

Such unforced majesty and scope of emotion in poems like 'The Building' and 'The Old Fools' have hardly been heard in English poetry since the great requiem of another romantic – Wilfred Owen's war poem 'Strange Meeting' – and about Owen Larkin wrote a moving tribute.

But his personality has no hint of Owen's priggishness. His sanity and pleasure are in very ordinary life and doings, about which he throws off phrases of devastating memorableness ('Glaring at jellies'; 'an awful pie'). No modern poet has been more free of cant – political, social, or literary – than Larkin. His humour and common sense are very like Barbara Pym's, whose novels he deeply admired, helping to rescue her in the 1960s (that ill-omened epoch) from the neglect of publishers convinced that her books were not at all the thing for a modern world. In neither artist is there any question of the 'major' or the 'minor', although neither would be likely to have been awarded the Nobel Prize. Both are completely though unpretentiously themselves, and, as the poet said of the novelist, in its art such an achievement 'will not diminish'.

17

Larkin's Voice

X. J. Kennedy

It had to be, in the end, a common cancer that bore off Philip Larkin. He could hardly have died with a flourish, like Saint-Exupéry, by charging off into the sky on a mission of reconnaissance only to vanish; or like Hemingway, by blowing out his brains. Nor could he go, like Matthew Arnold, in a burst of joy that stopped his heart in midair while leaping a fence to welcome a granddaughter. No, the dismal ordinariness of life, which Larkin so fondly celebrated, had to bring him down by its own dull strategies.

As a critic, to be sure, he delighted in being a curmudgeon. The gist of his message, given in his introduction to a sheaf of record reviews, *All What Jazz*, is that art, unless it helps us to enjoy and to endure, is nothing at all. In deliberately cultivating a stance of reaction – blaming Picasso for placing two eyes on the same side of a face, Henry Moore for perforating his figures, Samuel Beckett for setting out his actors with the trash – Larkin seems hardly a serious foe of modernity. But for the great modern artist's hordes of inferior imitators, he is a dangerous critic to meet in a dark alley. What refreshes in Larkin's complaint isn't its querulous tone, but its brash willingness to risk the charge of philistinism. Here, he implies, am I, a reasonably intelligent man willing to utter the worst doubts of the man in the street. And along with this trusty consumer, Larkin distrusts jazz that tends toward a shrill scream, the canvas that stays empty, the poem that in matter and form seems an accidental array of beard-mutterings.

Like John Betjeman, whom he admired, Larkin achieved a poetry from which even people who distrust poetry – most people – can take comfort and delight. Surely it is the poetry that seems his enduring testament: only 105 pages, not counting *The North Ship*, an early collection of Yeats-imitations that the author came to disparage. Yet what a monolith, those 105 pages! In it, Larkin performs the feat of transfixing drab, awful post-war

England: the seediness of Mr Bleaney's room, with its fusty bed
and a souvenir saucer in which to snuff out cigarettes, a window-
view of 'a strip of building land, / Tussocky, littered'. It is the run-
down boarding-house scene of *Lucky Jim*, whose anti-hero, the
cynical little twit pretending to be a scholar, Kingsley Amis is
supposed to have modelled after Larkin.

But Larkin was no Lucky Jim. Had Amis's Jim won the job of
University Librarian at Hull, he would quickly have sold the
library's Second Folio, replaced it with a facsimile, and taken off
with the proceeds to Aruba. Larkin stayed at his post for thirty
years, presiding over the transformation of a small provincial
library into a very nearly great one, increasing its collections
fourfold and directing a staff that grew from a dozen to more than
a hundred. He mounted a successful campaign to help Britain
hang on to its literary manuscript holdings. In life, he was a man
who shouldered with good grace crushing responsibility.

Still, it is the voice of some unlucky Jim that addresses us in
Larkin's best-known early poems: 'Toads', in which the speaker
wishes he might instantly blarney his way to fame, love and
money, but knows he won't; 'Poetry of Departures', with its
mingled envy and contempt for those who have 'chucked up
everything / And just cleared off'. Any of these poems follows an
order almost like a formula, as does the still more celebrated
'Church Going'. The speaker confesses himself torn between
two attractive and irreconcilable attitudes (faith and doubt, or
whatever), wrestles with an insoluble ethical dilemma, and in the
end imposes a quick solution on it. I like these poems, but not
nearly so well as certain other, deeply compassionate poems, in
which Unlucky Jim falls mute: 'Wedding-Wind', a marvellous act
of female mimicry, seemingly written to show that the poet can
imagine passionate fulfilment, if he so wants; or 'At Grass', that
superb evocation of old racehorses put out to pasture:

> Do memories plague their ears like flies?
> They shake their heads. Dusk brims the shadows.
> Summer by summer all stole away,
> The starting-gates, the crowds and cries –
> All but the unmolesting meadows.

That doesn't budge from memory. Nor does the wry and heartily
envious title poem of *The Whitsun Weddings*, with its affectionate

view of newly married proletarians; neither does 'An Arundel Tomb', 'Broadcast', nor in the last collection, *High Windows* of 1974, 'Vers de Société', that frank and funny meditation on the pleasures and pains of bachelor solitude, nor 'Cut Grass', a lyric that defies the reader's fear that nothing good can come of rhymes so trite (*breath / death, hours / flowers, June / strewn*). In what quiet triumph this last poem ends, with a view of

> White lilac bowed,
> Lost lanes of Queen Anne's lace,
> And that high-builded cloud
> Moving at summer's pace.

Clearly, these are stupendously well-made poems, sometimes pursuing patterns so ingenious that the reader is hardly aware of their ingenuity – the alliterative l-sounds there, the rhyme-schemes that seem worked out on a calculator. In all great metrical poets from Wyatt to Hardy, I suspect, there is an element of self-flagellation: of setting oneself impossible goals, and winning through to them at terrible cost in time, toil and spirit. In such poems, Larkin shows, I think, as keen a sense of rhyme as we can find in the work of any English-speaking poet; and, of all English and American poets of our time, perhaps rivalled only by Frost, he shows the best sense of the pulsebeat that resides in idioms. His language, however ordinary, is chosen brilliantly ('a snivel on the violins'[1]), and it is woven together so well that it seems not likely to unravel.

Unlike the typical American Orphic bard of the moment, Larkin never says, 'Behold! I am one hell of a brilliant visionary, and my life is the most important thing in the world – admire me, damn you, or die.' By contrast, the voice of Larkin, modest and clear and scrupulous, is that of a man who sees himself as just a bit silly: the amateur student of architecture who, entering a church, takes off his cycle-clips 'in awkward reverence'. In the end, I think, we love Larkin for admitting to a quality we recognise in ourselves – a certain dull contentment with our lives, for all their ignobility.

18

Philip Larkin, 1922–85

Donald Hall

Unless there is a cache of poems secreted somewhere in Hull, which we may doubt, the poet Philip Larkin died before the man. As far as I know, his last poem was 'Aubade', published in *The Times Literary Supplement* almost a decade ago. It begins:

> I work all day, and get half drunk at night.
> Waking at four to soundless dark, I stare.
> In time the curtain-edges will grow light.
> Till then I see what's really always there:
> Unresting death, a whole day nearer now,
> Making all thought impossible but how
> And where and when I shall myself die.

The fear of dying, daily companion of many, found its Homer, Dante, and Milton in Philip Larkin. His post-religious, almost Roman scepticism looks forward only to 'total emptiness for ever,/The sure extinction that we travel to'. As in his early 'Church Going', his language acknowledges religious feeling without diluting scepticism, sentimentalising loss, or asking for pity. Larkin is resolute, forthright, witty and gloomy. This is the man who famously said that deprivation was for him what daffodils were for Wordsworth. Yet surely the results of this life, in the shape of his poems, are gifts, not deprivations.

The Less Deceived announced Philip Larkin in 1955. As a young man he had published *The North Ship*, poems lyrical and Yeatsian and not yet Larkinesque. The early work resembled other young Englishmen: neo-Romantic, even a bit wet . . . . By the time I found him he had acquired Philip Larkin's voice. I heard him first on John Wain's BBC programme, 'New Soundings', in 1953 – where I also first heard Kingsley Amis telling about *Lucky Jim*.

Larkin's quality was clear; it was also clear that something new was happening. Although *The Less Deceived* was a small-press book – published by George Hartley who ran the Marvell Press and edited *Listen*, the best literary magazine of its time – it was published with a list of subscribers which included almost all English poets under forty: Amis, Bergonzi, Boyars, Brownjohn, Conquest, Davie, Enright, Hamburger, Hill, Jennings, MacBeth, Murphy, Thwaite, Tomlinson, Wain. (Thom Gunn was in California; Ted Hughes was not yet Ted Hughes.) And there were dons: Bateson, Dobrée, Dodsworth, Fraser, Kermode, Leishmann.

It was not long before Larkin became a popular poet in England, second only to Betjeman in public affection. When a good poet becomes popular there is always some silly reason as well as recognition of excellence. Dylan Thomas became a bestseller in this country – surely the obscurest poet ever to sell ten thousand copies – because tales of drunkenness and irreverence sold copies. With Robert Frost, the carefully cultivated rural manner – gussied up by the Luce publications untill he resembled Scattergood Baines – sold copies and had little to do with the real man.

With Larkin and his English readers, the silliness which helped to make him popular was his genuine, uncultivated, sincere philistinism. In his prose he wrote disparagingly of painters who put two noses on one face and sculptors who carved holes through bodies; he lectured us on the *ugliness* of modernism, most especially the three P's: Pound, Picasso and (Charlie) Parker. In the United States the terrorists of modernism have frightened the semi-educated middle class into accepting anything that carries the Avant-garde Seal of Approval. In England the middle classes are not so gullible; many remain secure in the conviction that Picasso is a fake, and that good painters can be defined as the ones who make horses that look like horses. When he made an anthology, Larkin's *Oxford Book of Twentieth-Century English Verse* was a monument to modesty and amateurism: Sir John Squire and yards of doggerel. Doubtless it is the *worst* anthology of modern poetry, with the possible exception of Yeats's . . .

Larkin's poetry of course is another matter. There is nothing modest or amateur about 'The Whitsun Weddings' or 'Aubade'. *The Less Deceived* was a superb volume, with three or four of Larkin's best poems and two dozen fine ones. Some are corny but splendidly achieved: 'At Grass' is the best horse picture ever painted. Back in the mid-1950s, the jocular and tough-minded 'Toads' stood out. Gradually, the softer and more ruminative 'Church Going' seems more to represent Larkin's best. In his second volume, *The Whitsun Weddings*, the title poem may be the finest moment in all his work. Characteristic in the place it is spoken from – a little to the side of life, watching, commenting – it is both empathetic and aloof, both superior and wistful. It ends:

> I thought of London spread out in the sun,
> Its postal districts packed like squares of wheat:
>
> There we were aimed. And as we raced across
>   Bright knots of rail
> Past standing Pullmans, walls of blackened moss
> Came close, and it was nearly done, this frail
> Travelling coincidence; and what it held
> Stood ready to be loosed with all the power
> That being changed can give. We slowed again,
> And as the tightened brakes took hold, there swelled
> A sense of falling, like an arrow-shower
> Sent out of sight, somewhere becoming rain.

Look at the way sentences curl down the page. Who else among us has made such motions?

The answer, I think, is Robert Frost, but I do not suggest direct influence. If there is influence, Frost to Larkin, it comes by way of Edward Thomas, whom Frost instructed. Although Thomas Hardy is Larkin's master – the only earlier twentieth-century poet clearly superior (and Geoffrey Hill the only contemporary) – the comparison with Frost remains useful. Frost loved to play the English sentence across the English line, usually pausing to rhyme on the way, mimicking what he called 'sentence sounds'. These sentence sounds show themselves by phrase-pitch and perform a sophistication of syntax. At the end of 'Mr Bleaney', from *The Whitsun Weddings*, we can see Larkin using the imitative gesture of syntax as well as Frost did it.

> But if he stood and watched the frigid wind
> Tousling the clouds, lay on the fusty bed
> Telling himself that this was home, and grinned,
> And shivered, without shaking off the dread
>
> That how we live measures our own nature,
> And at his age having no more to show

> Than one hired box should make him pretty sure
> He warranted no better, I don't know.

This awkward, difficult-to-say sentence mimics the reluctance of the mind to reach conclusion about its own worth or lack of worth. The muscular gestures of its hesitation expresses, by form and mimickry of grammar, the state of mind that the language describes. In this coincidence of manner and matter is a good portion of Larkin's genius.

But not only here. In an interview Larkin spoke about his reputation as a melancholy man, and protested that he thought he was rather funny, actually. True enough: 'Sexual intercourse began / In nineteen-sixty three / (Which was rather late for me) – / Between the end of the *Chatterley* ban / And the Beatles' first LP'. But something besides humour redeems the gloom of Philip Larkin. His poetry is beautiful, which gives us deep and abiding pleasure, however melancholy a paraphrase may be. At the end of 'Aubade', Larkin makes a metaphor, appropriately sinister, in a gorgeous pentameter line:

> Meanwhile telephones crouch, getting ready to ring
> In locked-up offices, and all the uncaring
> Intricate rented world begins to rouse.
> The sky is white as clay, with no sun.
> Work has to be done.
> Postmen like doctors go from house to house.

Doubtless the poem is *deprived* enough . . . but if you don't walk out of the theatre humming the tune, you don't read poetry.

Notes

PREFACE

1. B. C. Bloomfield, 'Obituary: Philip Arthur Larkin', *Library Association Record*, vol. LXXXVIII (Jan. 1986) p. 19.
2. Larkin to Dale Salwak, 20 Sep. 1985.
3. Kingsley Amis, 'Professor Philip Larkin', *University of Hull Bulletin*, 16 Jan. 1986, p. 4.
4. Paul De Angelis on the occasion of a 'Celebration of Barbara Pym', held at the Gramercy Park Hotel, New York, 3 Oct. 1984.

CHAPTER 1. FAREWELL TO A FRIEND
Kingsley Amis

1. What follows was written to order for the *Observer* within a week of Philip Larkin's death.

CHAPTER 2. LARKIN'S OXFORD
Anthony Curtis

1. Philip Larkin, *Required Writing* (London: Faber and Faber, 1983; New York: Farrar, Straus and Giroux, 1984) p. 23.
2. John Betjeman, *An Oxford University Chest* (London: J. Miles, 1938).
3. Larkin, *Jill*, p. 228.
4. Philip Larkin, 'Not the Place's Fault', first published in *Umbrella* (Spring 1959) and included in *An Enormous Yes: In Memoriam Philip Larkin (1922–1985)*, ed. Harry Chambers (Cornwall: Peterloo Poets, 1986) p. 52.
5. Philip Larkin, 'The Traffic in the Distance', in *Required Writing*, p. 274. Larkin acknowledged his debt to Hall in an interview in *Tracks*, vol. I (Summer 1967) pp. 5–10.
6. Julian Hall, *The Senior Commoner* (London: Victor Gollancz, 1933) p. 119.
7. The connection was observed by Pat Dale Scrimegeour in 'Philip Larkin's "Dockery and Son" and Julian Hall's *The Senior Commoner*', *Notes and Queries*. vol. n.s. XXXIII (June 1986) p. 193.
8. Gavin Bone, *Beowulf in Modern Verse, with an Essay and Pictures* (Oxford: Basil Blackwell, 1945) p. v. The words are from the Preface by G. H. B., Bone's parent.
9. Ian Davie's published works include *Aviator Loquitor* (London: Fortune Press, 1943) and *Piers Prodigal* (London: Harvill, 1961) and *Roman*

Pentecost (London: Hamish Hamilton, 1970). He also edited *Oxford Poetry, 1942–1943* (Oxford: Blackwell, 1943).

10. William Bell, *Elegies* (London, n.d.) and *Mountains Beneath the Horizon* (London: Faber and Faber, 1950).

11. Both of these anthologies were published by R. A. Caton's Fortune Press, London, as were early collections of verse by Bell, Davie and Larkin. No one ever made a fortune through publishing with the Press, but many poets went away to the war knowing that their work was safely in print between stiff covers.

12. Michael Meyer, 'John Heath-Stubbs in the Forties', *Aquarius*, vol. x (Winter 1978) p. 10.

13. B. C. Bloomfield, *Philip Larkin: A Bibliography, 1933–1976* (London: Faber, 1980) to which all Larkin scholars are deeply indebted.

14. Sidney Keyes and Michael Meyer (eds), *Eight Oxford Poets* (London: Routledge, 1941). The anthology was rejected by T. S. Eliot at Faber, but accepted by Herbert Read acting as poetry advisor for Routledge (Meyer, 'John Heath-Stubbs in the Forties', p. 12).

15. Ibid., p. 12.

16. See Larkin, *Required Writing*, pp. 19–21.

17. In conversation with the present writer.

18. See Larkin's 'Introduction' to *Jill* (London: Fortune Press, 1946; Faber and Faber, 1964, 1975; New York: Overlook Press, 1976); and for Wain's memories of Oxford *c.* 1944 see *Sprightly Running: Part of an Autobiography* (London: Macmillan, 1962) and the chapter on Nevil Coghill in *Dear Shadows: Portraits from Memory* (London: Macmillan, 1986).

19. Larkin, *Required Writing*, p. 24.

CHAPTER 4.   'I REMEMBER, I REMEMBER', 1955–85
Maeve M. Brennan

1. E. R. Braithwaite, *To Sir, With Love* (London: Bodley Head, 1959).

2. *Listen*, vols 1–3 (Hessle: Marvell Press, 1954–60).

3. Philip Larkin, 'Sad Steps', *High Windows* (London: Faber and Faber; New York: Farrar Straus and Giroux, 1974) p. 32.

4. Philip Larkin, *'A Lifted Study-Storehouse': The Brynmor Jones Library, 1929–1979*, updated to 1985 with an Appreciation of Philip Larkin as Librarian by Maeve Brennan (Hull: Hull University Press, 1987; Philip Larkin Memorial Series no. 1) p. 9.

5. Larkin, *Required Writing*, p. 57.

6. Philip Larkin, 'Dockery and Son', *The Whitsun Weddings* (London and Boston, Mass.: Faber and Faber, 1964) p. 38.

7. Philip Larkin, 'The Building', *High Windows*, p. 26.

8. William Shakespeare, 'Sonnet no. 18', ll. 11–14 (London: Thorpe, 1609).

CHAPTER 5. 'GOODBYE, WITHERSPOON': A JAZZ FRIENDSHIP
John White

1. Larkin to John White, 5 May 1983.
2. Philip Larkin, 'Crows and Daws', *The American Scholar*, 51 (Spring 1982) p. 290.
3. Ibid., pp. 288–9.
4. Philip Larkin, *All What Jazz: A Record Diary, 1961–68* (London: Faber and Faber; New York: St Martin's Press, 1970, 1985) p. 290.
5. Larkin to John White, 8 May 1985.
6. Larkin to John White, 1 Oct. 1984.
7. Larkin to John White, 25 Nov. 1984.
8. Larkin, *All What Jazz*, p. 127.
9. Ibid., p. 131.
10. Ibid., p. 157.
11. Ibid., p. 196.
12. Ibid., p. 226.
13. Philip Larkin, 'Here', *The Whitsun Weddings*, p. 9.
14. Larkin, *All What Jazz*, p. 45.
15. Steve Voce, 'It Don't Mean a Thing', *Jazz Journal International*, vol. xxxix (Jan 1986) p. 9.
16. Ibid.
17. Larkin, *All What Jazz*, p. 41.

CHAPTER 6. PHILIP LARKIN ABROAD
Janice Rossen

1. Larkin, *Required Writing*, p. 55.
2. Larkin to Barbara Pym, PYM 151, fol. 51, dated 11 Sep. 1968. Hereafter numbers prefixed PYM are items in the collection of Barbara Pym's papers lodged at the Bodleian Library, Oxford.
3. PYM 151, fol. 72, 18 July 1971.
4. PYM 151, fol. 26, 7 Dec. 1963.
5. PYM 152, fol. 33, 21 Aug. 1978.
6. Larkin, *Required Writing*, p. 55.
7. Larkin to John Betjeman, 25 Feb. 1976. Lodged in the University of Victoria Library.
8. PYM 151, fol. 119, 28 Nov. 1976.
9. PYM 152, fol. 51, 14 Dec. 1979.
10. Larkin, *Required Writing*, p. 65.
11. Ibid., p. 54.
12. Ibid.
13. Conversation with Maeve Brennan, Former Sub-Librarian, and Brian Dyson, Archivist, Brynmor Jones Library.
14. PYM 151, fol. 27, 7 Dec. 1963.
15. Andrew Motion, *Philip Larkin* (London: Methuen, 1982) p. 19.
16. Larkin, *Required Writing*, p. 55.

CHAPTER 7. AN INNOCENT AT HOME
Noel Hughes

1. Larkin, *Required Writing*, p. 55.
2. Ibid., p. 47.

CHAPTER 8. PHILIP LARKIN AND BARBARA PYM:
TWO QUIET PEOPLE
Hazel Holt

1. Pym to Larkin, 15 Apr., and Larkin to Pym, 17 Apr. 1975.
2. Philip Larkin, 'Reputations Revisited', *The Times Literary Supplement*, 21 Jan. 1977, pp. 66–7.
3. Philip Larkin, 'Foreword' to Barbara Pym, *An Unsuitable Attachment* (London: Macmillan; New York: E. P. Dutton, 1982) p. 5. Reprinted as 'The Rejection of Barbara Pym', in *The Life and Work of Barbara Pym*, ed. Dale Salwak (London: Macmillan; Iowa City: University of Iowa Press, 1987) p. 171.
4. Larkin to Pym, 15 July 1963.
5. Larkin to Pym, 20 May 1963, 3 Feb 1970, 29 May 1971, 14 July 1964.
6. Larkin to Pym, 22 Feb 1977.
7. Pym to Larkin, 4 Mar 1977.
8. Larkin to Pym, 29 Oct 1977.
9. Larkin to Pym, 20 Sep 1977.
10. Pym to Larkin, 28 Oct 1979.
11. Pym to Larkin, 7 Apr 1964.
12. Larkin to Pym, 1 Oct and 18 Nov 1961.
13. Larkin to Pym, 15 July 1963, 8 Oct 1969, 13 Jan 1967, 5 June 1974, 22 Jan 1975.
14. Pym to Larkin, 12 Jan and 14 Sep 1964.
15. Larkin to Pym, 13 Jan and 3 Oct 1967, 18 Mar 1969.
16. Pym diary entry, 20 Aug 1968.
17. Larkin to Pym, 8 Apr 1963, 8 Oct 1969, 30 Aug 1965.
18. Larkin to Pym, 8 Apr 1963, 8 Oct 1969, 1 Nov 1979.
19. Pym to Larkin, 3 Nov 1963, and Larkin to Pym, 7 Dec 1963.
20. Pym to Larkin, 29 Jan 1978.
21. Larkin to Pym, 7 Jan 1965.
22. Pym diary entry, 23 Apr 1977.
23. Pym to Larkin, 15 Mar 1979.
24. Larkin to Pym, 18 July 1971.
25. Larkin to Hazel Holt, 29 Apr 1984.

CHAPTER 9. LARKIN'S PRESENCE
William H. Pritchard

1. Larkin, *Required Writing*, pp. 53–4.
2. Ibid., p. 194.

3. *Selected Prose of Robert Frost*, ed. Hyde Cox and Edward Connery Lathem (New York: Collier Books, 1968) p. 18.
4. Larkin, *Required Writing*, p. 67.
5. *Randall Jarrell's Letters*, ed. Mary Jarrell (Boston, Mass.: Houghton-Mifflin, 1985) p. 394.
6. Calvin Bedient, 'Philip Larkin', in *Eight Contemporary Poets* (London: Oxford University Press, 1974) p. 94.
7. John Bayley, *Selected Essays* (Cambridge: Cambridge University Press, 1984) p. 96.
8. Larkin, *Required Writing*, p. 47.
9. Ibid., p. 22.
10. Ibid., p. 50.
11. Philip Larkin, 'Louis MacNeice', *New Statesman*, 6 Sep 1963, p. 294.
12. Randall Jarrell, 'Poet, Critics, and Readers', in *Kipling, Auden & Co.: Essays and Reviews, 1935–1964* (New York: Farrar, Straus and Giroux, 1980) p. 316.
13. Robert Frost, 'Carpe Diem', in *The Poetry of Robert Frost*, ed. Edward Connery Lathem (New York: Holt, Rinehart and Winston, 1972) p. 335.
14. Lowell to Jarrell, 11 Oct 1957.
15. A. Alvarez, *Beyond All This Fiddle* (New York: Random House, 1968) p. 81.
16. Andrew Motion, 'This is Your Subject Speaking', *The Times Literary Supplement*, 2 July 1986, p. 143.
17. Larkin, *Required Writing*, p. 75.
18. James Dickey, *Sorties* (Baton Rouge, LA: Louisiana State University Press, 1971) p. 89.
19. Larkin, *Required Writing*, p. 174.
20. Ibid., p. 70.
21. *British and American Poets: Chaucer to the Present*, ed. W. Jackson Bates and David Perkins (New York: Harcourt Brace Jovanovich, 1986) p. 900.
22. *Randall Jarrell's Letters*, p. 413.
23. Brad Leithauser, 'America's Master of Former Verse', *The New Republic*, 24 Mar 1982, p. 16.

CHAPTER 10.   PHILIP LARKIN: VOICES AND VALUES
J. R. Watson

1. Larkin, *Required Writing*, p. 140.
2. Ibid., p. 138.
3. Bill Ruddick, ' "Some ruin-bibber, randy for antique": Philip Larkin's Response to the Poetry of John Betjeman', *Critical Quarterly*, vol. xxviii (Winter 1986) pp. 63–9.
4. William Wordsworth, 'Preface' to *Lyrical Ballads*.
5. Philip Larkin, *Le Nozze di Pentecoste*, trs. Renato Oliva and Camillo Pennati (Torino, 1969) p. 115.
6. Charles Salter, 'Unusual Words Beginning with "un", "en", "out",

"up" and "on", in Thomas Hardy's Verse', *Victorian Poetry*, vol. XI (Winter 1973) pp. 257–61.

7. Seamus Heaney, 'Englands of the Mind', in *Preoccupations: Selected Prose, 1968–1978* (London: Faber and Faber, 1980), esp. p. 150.

8. Roland Barthes, *Writing Degree Zero*, trs. Annette Lavers and Colin Smith (New York: Harcourt, Brace and World, 1968) pp. 10–11.

9. Ibid.

10. Larkin, *Required Writing*, p. 87.

11. Larkin, 'Introduction' to *All What Jazz*, p. 293.

12. Larkin, *Required Writing*, p. 136.

13. Francis Berry, *Poetry and the Physical Voice* (London: Faber and Faber, 1962) pp. 102–3.

14. See Franklin R. Rogers, *Painting and Poetry, Form, Metaphor and the Language of Literature* (Lewisburg: Bucknell University Press, 1985) for a discussion of metaphor and the visual perception.

15. Berry, *Poetry and the Physical Voice*, p. 101.

16. R. P. Draper, *Lyric Tragedy* (London: Routledge and Kegan Paul, 1985) p. 214.

17. From a letter to Gavin Ewart, 26 July 1985. Reprinted by kind permission of Mr Ewart.

18. Barthes, *Writing Degree Zero*, pp. 10–11.

19. Barbara Everett, *Poets in their Time: Essays on English Poetry from Donne to Larkin* (London: Faber and Faber, 1986) p. 245. There are two fine essays on Larkin in this book; this quotation is taken from the second of them, 'Larkin's Edens'.

20. J. R. Watson, 'The Other Larkin', *Critical Quarterly*, vol. XVII (Winter 1975) pp. 347–60.

CHAPTER 11.   TENTATIVE INITIATION IN THE POETRY
John H. Augustine

1. Joseph Epstein, 'Miss Pym and Mr Larkin', *Commentary*, vol. LXVI (July 1986) p. 45.

2. Bruce K. Martin, *Philip Larkin*, ed. Kinley E. Roby (Boston, Mass.: Twayne, 1978) p. 45.

3. Mordecai Marcus, 'What is an Initiation Story?', in Isaac Sequeira's *The Theme of Initiation in Modern American Fiction* (Mysore, India: Geetha Book House, 1975) p. 20. Originally published in *The Journal of Aesthetics and Art Criticism*, vol. XIX (1960) pp. 221–8.

CHAPTER 12.   PHILIP LARKIN: THE METONYMIC MUSE
David Lodge

1. What follows is a chapter from my book, *The Modes of Modern Writing: Metaphor, Metonymy and the Typology of Modern Literature* (London: Edward Arnold, 1977; New York: Cornell University Press, 1977),

and a word of explanation about the theory on which it is based may be appropriate.

In the concluding pages of his paper entitled 'Two Aspects of Language and Two Types of Aphasic Disturbances' (Roman Jakobson and Morris Halle, *Fundamentals of Language* [The Hague, 1956]), Roman Jakobson, one of the founding fathers of Structuralism, expounded a distinction between metaphor and metonymy as the two 'poles' of all discourse. Language, like any system of signs, has a twofold character, involving two distinct operations, selection and combination. To produce a sentence like 'ships crossed the sea' (the example is my own, not Jakobson's) I *select* the words I need from the paradigms of the English language and *combine* them according to the rules of that language (subject–verb–object). If I substitute 'ploughed' for 'crossed', I create a *metaphor* based on a perceived similarity between two things otherwise different – the movement of a ship through water and the movement of a plough through the earth. If I substitute 'keels' for 'ships', I have used the figure of *synecdoche* (part standing for whole, or whole for part). If I substitute 'deep' for 'sea', I have used the figure of *metonymy* (an attribute or cause or effect of a thing standing for the thing itself). According to Jakobson, synecdoche is a subspecies of metonymy, since both are derived from *contiguity* and the *combination* axis of language, in contrast to metaphor, which derives from *similarity* and the *selection* axis. Jakobson takes these two rhetorical figures as models of the way whole discourses are constructed:

> The development of a discourse may take place along two different semantic lines: one topic may lead to another either through their similarity or their contiguity. The metaphorical way would be the more appropriate term for the first case, and the metonymic for the second, since they find their most condensed expression in metaphor and metonymy respectively. . . . In normal verbal behaviour both processes are continually operative, but careful observation will reveal that under the influence of a cultural pattern, personality, and verbal style, preference is given to one of the two processes over the other (p. 76)

2. See Iris Murdoch's essay, 'Against Dryness', *Encounter*, vol. xvi (Jan 1961) pp. 16–20.
3. In his introduction to the first important Movement anthology, *New Lines* (1956), Robert Conquest named Orwell as a major influence on these poets. Orwell's influence is even more evident in the fiction and criticism of the 1950s writers, especially John Wain's.
4. David Lodge, 'The Modern, the Contemporary and the Importance of Being Amis', in *Language of Fiction* (London: Routledge and Kegan Paul; New York: Columbia University Press, 1966, 1979) pp. 243–67.
5. Quoted in David Timms, *Philip Larkin* (Edinburgh: Oliver, 1973) pp. 60, 109.
6. Ibid., p. 21.

7. Ibid., p. 62.
8. Ibid., p. 112.
9. Philip Larkin, 'Coming', in *The Less Deceived* (London: Marvell Press, 1955) p. 17.
10. Quoted in Timms, *Philip Larkin*, p. 61.
11. Wordsworth, 'Preface' to *The Lyrical Ballads, 1798–1805*, ed. George Samson.
12. 'Larkin instructed Anthony Thwaite, then a radio producer, that the poem should be read holding a carefully sustained note until the very end, when it should "lift off the ground"', according to Timms' *Philip Larkin* (p. 120).

CHAPTER 13. ART AND LARKIN
Barbara Everett

1. What follows is the latter half of an essay on the friendship of Philip Larkin and Kingsley Amis, and particularly on the literary principles shared by both.
2. Alan Brownjohn, 'The Deep Blue Air', *The New Statesman*, 14 June 1974, pp. 854, 856.
3. Kingsley Amis, *Take A Girl Like You* (London: Victor Gollancz; New York: Harcourt, Brace and World, 1960) pp. 221–2.

CHAPTER 14. LARKIN'S HUMANITY VIEWED FROM ABROAD
Bruce K. Martin

1. John Wain, 'The Importance of Philip Larkin', *The American Scholar*, vol. LV (Spring 1986) p. 349.
2. See, for example, Motion, *Philip Larkin*, pp. 73–81.
3. Aristotle, *The Poetics*, IX, trs. S. H. Butcher.
4. Larkin, *Required Writing*, p. 121.
5. Aristotle, *The Poetics*, VIII.

CHAPTER 16. PHILIP LARKIN'S INNER WORLD
John Bayley

1. Larkin, *Required Writing*, p. 205.
2. Ibid., p. 47.

CHAPTER 17. LARKIN'S VOICE
X. J. Kennedy

1. Philip Larkin, 'Broadcast', *The Whitsun Weddings'*, p. 14.

Select Bibliography

PRIMARY SOURCES

Poetry collections

The North Ship (London: Fortune Press, 1945; London and Boston, Mass.: Faber and Faber, 1966).

XX Poems (privately printed in a limited edition of 100 copies, Belfast, 1951).

The Fantasy Poets: Philip Larkin (Swineford: Fantasy Press, 1954).

The Less Deceived (London: Marvell Press, 1955).

The Whitsun Weddings (London and Boston, Mass.: Faber and Faber, 1964).

High Windows (London: Faber and Faber; New York: Farrar, Straus and Giroux, 1974).

Femmes Damnées, Sycamore Broadsheet no. 27 (Oxford: Sycamore Press, 1978).

Novels

Jill (London: Fortune Press, 1946; Faber and Faber, 1964, 1975; New York: Overlook Press, 1976).

A Girl in Winter (London: Faber and Faber, 1947, 1975; New York: Overlook Press, 1976).

Prose non-fiction

All What Jazz: A Record Diary, 1961–68 (London: Faber and Faber; New York: St Martin's Press, 1970, 1985).

Required Writing: Miscellaneous Pieces, 1955–1982 (London: Faber and Faber, 1983; New York: Farrar, Straus and Giroux, 1984).

Works edited, or with contributions, by Philip Larkin

Oxford Poetry, 1942–1943, ed. Ian Davie (Oxford: Blackwell, 1943).

Poetry from Oxford in Wartime, ed. William Bell (London: Fortune Press, 1945).

Poetry of the 1950s, ed. D. J. Enright (Tokyo: Kenkyusha Press, 1955).

New Lines, ed. Robert Conquest (London: Macmillan, 1956).

Poet's Choice, ed. Paul Engle and Joseph Langland (New York: Dial Press, 1962).

The Oxford Book of Twentieth-Century English Verse, ed. Philip Larkin (Oxford: Clarendon Press, 1973).

The Arts Council Collection of Modern Literary Manuscripts, 1963–1972, ed. Jenny Stratford (London: Turret Books, 1974).

Interviews

'Four Young Poets, I. Philip Larkin', *The Times Educational Supplement*, 13 July 1956, p. 933.

'Speaking of Writing: XIII', *The Times*, 20 Feb 1964, p. 16.

'Four Conversations' (interviewer Ian Hamilton), *London Magazine*, vol. IV (1964) pp. 71–7; reprinted as 'Interviews with Philip Larkin and Christopher Middleton', in *Twentieth-Century Poetry*, ed. Graham Martin and P. N. Furbank (London: Open University Press, 1975).

'A Poet on the 8.15' (interviewer John Horder), *Manchester Guardian*, 20 May 1968, p. 9.

'The Unsung Gold Medallist' (interviewer Philip Oakes), *The Sunday Times Magazine*, 27 Mar 1966, pp. 63–5.

'A Conversation with Philip Larkin', *Tracks*, vol. I (1967) pp. 5–10.

'A Sharp-Edged View' (interviewer Frances Hill), *The Times Educational Supplement*, 19 May 1972, p. 19.

'A Great Parade of Single Poems: Interview with Anthony Thwaite', *The Listener*, 12 Apr 1973, pp. 472–4.

'Philip Larkin – A Profile' (interviewer Dan Jacobson), *New Review*, vol. I (1974) pp. 25–8.

'A Voice for Our Time' (interviewer Miriam Gross), *The Observer*, 16 Dec 1979, p. 35; reprinted as 'An Interview with the *Observer*', in Larkin, *Required Writing*, pp. 47–56.

'The True and the Beautiful: a conversation with Philip Larkin' (interviewer John Haffenden), *London Magazine*, vol. XX (1980) pp. 81–95; reprinted in his *Viewpoints: Poets in Conversation* (London: Faber and Faber, 1981).

'The Art of Poetry, XXX: Philip Larkin' (interviewer Robert Phillips), *Paris Review*, vol. 84 (1982) pp. 42–72; reprinted as 'An Interview with *Paris Review*', in Larkin, *Required Writing*, pp. 57–76.

SECONDARY SOURCES

Bibliography

Bloomfield, B. C., *Philip Larkin: A Bibliography* (London: Faber and Faber, 1980).

Tierce, Mike, 'Philip Larkin: Secondary Sources, 1950–1984', *Bulletin of Bibliography*, vol. XXXIII (1985) pp. 67–75.

Dyson, Brian, *et al.* (eds), *Philip Larkin: His Life and Work* (Hull: Brynmor Jones Library, 1986).

Essays and books (since 1984)

Amis, Kingsley, 'Professor Philip Larkin', *University of Hull Bulletin*, 16 Jan 1986, p. 4.

Amis, Martin, 'Memento Mori', *Vanity Fair*, vol. IL (1986) pp. 46–7.

Beatty, Jack, 'The Country's Changing Measure', *Atlantic*, vol. CCLVII (1986) p. 15.

Bloomfield, B. C., 'Obituary: Philip Arthur Larkin', *Library Association Record*, vol. 88 (Jan 1986) p. 19.

Brownjohn, Alan, 'Poet Who Reluctantly Came to the Point', *The Listener*, 13 Feb 1986, pp. 15–16.

Davis, Clive, 'Convivial Recluse', *Yorkshire Post*, 3 Dec 1985, p. 1.

Davis, Elizabeth, 'Gravity and the Sea: "Church Going" and "Next, Please"', *Publication of the Arkansas Philological Association*, vol. xi (1985) pp. 17–23.

Enright, D. J., 'Best Laureate We Never Had?', *Yorkshire Post*, 3 Dec 1985, p. 1.

Epstein, Joseph, 'Miss Pym and Mr Larkin', *Commentary*, vol. xxcii (1986) p. 38.

Everett, Barbara, *Poets in their Time: Essays on English Poetry from Donne to Larkin* (London: Faber and Faber, 1986).

Ezard, John, 'Larkin, the Romantic Recluse, Dies at 63', *Guardian*, 3 Dec 1985, pp. 1, 6.

——, 'University Exhibition Helps Fill Vacuum Left by Larkin', *Guardian*, 2 June 1986, p. 2.

——, 'Valentine Farewell to Larkin in Jazz Elegy', *Guardian*, 15 Feb 1986, pp. 1, 15.

Garland, Patrick, 'Filming with Philip Larkin: "Colourful, balding, book-basher"', *The Listener*, 12 Dec 1985, p. 22.

Hadwin, Sara, 'Larkin: Great Poet, Great Man', *Daily Mail*, 3 Dec 1985, p. 1.

——, 'Literary Treasure Trove of the Young Poet Larkin', *Hull Daily Mail*, 22 Sep 1986, p. 6.

Hamilton, Alan, 'Larkin's Unpublished Writings Saved', *The Times*, 1 Aug 1986, p. 3.

Hamilton, Ian, 'Philip Larkin, 1922–1985', *The Sunday Times*, 8 Dec 1985, p. 34.

Harvey, Geoffrey, *The Renaissance Tradition in Modern English Poetry: Rhetoric and Experiences* (London: Macmillan, 1986).

Holloway, David, 'Philip Larkin, the Poet Who Found Fame with Small Output', *Daily Telegraph*, 3 Dec 1985, p. 13.

Latre, Guido, *Locking Earth to the Sky: A Structuralist Approach to Philip Larkin's Poetry* (Frankfurt-am-Main: Peter Long, 1985).

Levi, Peter, 'The English Wisdom of a Master Poet', *Sunday Telegraph*, 8 Dec 1985, p. 9.

'Literary World Pays Respects to Hull Poet', *Daily Mail*, 15 Feb 1986, p. 3.

Moon, Brenda E., 'Obituary: Philip Arthur Larkin', *Library Association Record*, vol. lxxxviii (1986) p. 19.

Morrison, Blake, 'Unrequired Writing', *Observer*, 8 Dec 1985, p. 2.

'Obituary: Mr Philip Larkin: Poet of Reticence and Restraint', *The Times*, 3 Dec 1985, p. 16.

Osborne, John, 'Philip Larkin (1922–1985)', *Arts Diary*, Mar–Apr 1986, pp. 6–7.

'Peterborough', 'Nonsense Verse', *Daily Telegraph*, 3 Dec 1985, p. 12.

'Philip Larkin is Dead at 63', *New York Times*, 3 Dec 1985, pp. 11–12.

'Philip Larkin, RIP', *National Review*, 31 Jan 1986, p. 25.

Pritchard, William H., 'The Least Deceived: Philip Larkin, Poet of Death', *New Republic*, 6 Jan 1986, pp. 41–2.

Reibetanz, John, 'Lyric Poetry as Self-Possession: Philip Larkin', *University of Toronto Quarterly*, vol. LIV (1985) pp. 265–83.

Sharrock, Roger, 'Private Faces in Public Places: the Poetry of Larkin and Lowell', *English*, vol. XXXVI (1987) pp. 113–32.

Wain, John, 'The Importance of Philip Larkin', *The American Scholar*, vol. LV (1986) pp. 349–64.

Wheen, Francis, 'Weep for Adonis, for He Was Tory', *New Statesman*, 22 Dec 1985, p. 14.

Whitsitt, Julia, '"When Disbelief Has Gone": the Personal and Societal Past in Philip Larkin's Poetry', *Lamar Journal of the Humanities*, vol. XI (1985) pp. 27–32.

Index